Corporate
Community Relations

Corporate Community Relations

The Principle of the Neighbor of Choice

Edmund M. Burke

Foreword by Raymond V. Gilmartin

QUORUM BOOKS
Westport, Connecticut • London

Library of Congress Cataloging-in-Publication Data

Burke, Edmund M.
   Corporate community relations : the principle of the
neighbor of choice / Edmund M. Burke ; foreword by
Raymond V. Gilmartin.
       p.   cm.
   Includes bibliographical references and indexes.
   ISBN 1–56720–192–X (alk. paper)
   1. Corporate image.   2. Social responsibility of
business.   3. Public relations.   I. Title.
   HD59.2.B87   1999
   658.4'08—dc21   98–27837

British Library Cataloguing in Publication Data is available.

A paperback edition of *Corporate Community Relations* is available from
Praeger Publishers, an imprint of Greenwood Publishing Group, Inc.
(ISBN 0–275–96471–X).

Library of Congress Catalog Card Number: 98–27837
ISBN: 1–56720–192–X

First published in 1999

Quorum Books, 88 Post Road West, Westport, CT 06881
An imprint of Greenwood Publishing Group, Inc.

Printed in the United States of America

⊗™

The paper used in this book complies with the
Permanent Paper Standard issued by the National
Information Standards Organization (Z39.48–1984).

10 9 8 7 6 5 4 3 2 1

To the Rev. J. Donald Monan, S.J.,
Chancellor and former President of Boston College,
who shared the vision of The Center for Corporate
Community Relations, and to Nancy Goldberg,
who helped make the vision a reality.

Contents

IV. The Social Vision

Foreword: Why Merck Wants to Be a Neighbor of Choice

At Merck our business is to respond to society's needs for important medicines and vaccines. This the foundation of everything we do.

In 1950, George W. Merck, our modern-day founder, expressed a belief that reflects our operating philosophy to this day. He said, "We try to remember that medicine is for the patient. We try never to forget that medicine is for people. Not for the profits. The profits will follow, and if we have remembered that, they have never failed to appear."

This approach has guided us in discovering, developing, manufacturing, and marketing breakthrough medicines that prevent disease and enhance the quality of life for millions of people around the world. It also guides the way we conduct our business in the communities where we operate.

Neighbor of choice is consistent with our mission and operating philosophy. We agree with Dr. Burke that basing relationships on trust and respect leads to more lasting and constructive interactions with the vital forces of society.

We recognize that trust has to be earned. It is by providing an excellent work environment that we earn the loyalty of our employees; by developing innovative medicines that customers see our products as adding value to their lives; and by committing to practices that protect our neighbors and the environment that we earn their acceptance and license to operate.

Trust, however, is not granted to us just because we pay our share of taxes or hire residents to work in our company. While that may have been the case at one time, it is not the only criterion today. People expect us to become partners in solving community problems. They want the private sector to support programs and institutions that improve the quality of community life.

That is why we have adopted the principle of neighbor of choice. It is a metaphor that accurately depicts how we want to be positioned in our communities. We want our communities to be proud of Merck. We want to be seen as integral constructive members of the communities in which we operate.

We believe this approach to community relations produces an atmosphere where businesses and communities can work together and prosper.

Raymond V. Gilmartin
Chairman, President, & Chief Executive Officer
Merck & Co., Inc.

Acknowledgments

While I am responsible for the material in this book—its facts, recommendations, and theme—it could not have been written without the help of many people. I would like to acknowledge the support and encouragement of the staff at The Boston College Center for Corporate Community Relations. I am especially indebted to Lisa Rogers, who read all the drafts and provided editorial suggestions. Steve Rochlin, Susan Thomas, and Bradley Googins offered expert comments and much needed advice. Cheryl Yaffe Kiser gave me excellent design suggestions. Michael Stevenson provided library assistance. Patrice Russell and Andrew Rollauer provided invaluable assistance in creating the figures for the book.

In particular, I need to acknowledge the support of Nancy Goldberg, who not only offered her insightful advice, original ideas, constructive comments, and thoughtful criticism, most of which found its way into this book. She also gave me the encouragement and enthusiasm needed to write this book. She had a lot to do with helping me form the ideas that led to the development of the neighbor of choice concept. I could not have written this book without her advice.

I am also indebted to those who provided the beginning support for the Boston College Center for Corporate Community Relations, which provided the forum for learning about a newly emerging function in business. June Gary Hopps, Dean of the Graduate School of Social Work at Boston College, provided the seed money to start The Center's first institutes. Many community relations and public affairs managers offered advice, guidance, and, most of all, encouragement to start a center on community relations.

My wife, Lee, provided not only inspiration for the book; she was also the source of the information about the psychological contract. She gave me a critical understanding of the concept and its applicability to corporations and communities.

In addition, this book could not have been written without the comments, thoughts, and reactions of the thousands of corporate community relations executives who have attended the courses, workshops, and seminars I have taught since 1983. Their observations have served as a reality check to the principles explained in this book, and they have been instrumental in the formation of the neighbor of choice principle. I also apologize for subjecting them to what sometimes has been a work in progress. They have been part of an experiment, often unwittingly. I am exceedingly grateful for their part in helping me write this book. It is as much theirs as it is mine.

Introduction: The New Expectations of Today's Corporate Communities

On June 10, 1995, Shell Oil Co. in the United Kingdom began towing a used oil rig, commissioned Brent Spar, out into the North Atlantic to sink it. The company arrived at the deep-water disposal decision after four years of environmental studies, reports, and observations by scientists (including a Nobel Prize winner), consultants, and universities. Government officials from regulators to the prime minister of Great Britain approved and supported the decision.

But environmental activists led by Greenpeace whipped up community sentiment against the company and brought a halt to Shell's plans ten days later. The company was forced to move the rig to a Norwegian fjord while it made contingency plans for disposing of it on dry land.

The costs to the company? Incalculable. At the very least, Shell estimates that it cost an additional $200 million just to change the disposal decision. In addition, boycotts and threats against service stations caused huge losses in sales. In one week alone boycotts in Germany caused sales of Shell products to drop 50 percent. Fifty Shell service stations were vandalized, two firebombed, and one raked with bullets.

The company's image as an environmental leader in the oil industry, admits Shell's managing director Heinz Rothermund, was damaged severely. Its reputation as a company was shattered, causing employee morale to plummet.

Almost a month later, on July 27, phosphorous trichloride leaked from Merck's Flint River pharmaceutical plant in Albany, Georgia. The leak produced a clearly visible toxic cloud above the plant just as a TV crew was driving by. Forty-five people were taken to hospitals, and 400 workers were evacuated.

The TV reporters quickly began reporting on the incident and interviewing nearby residents, one of whom was the director of a day care center. The potential for damage to Merck's image and its ability to operate was great, but to the surprise of the reporters, the community response was nonchalantly indifferent and, in some cases, laudatory. Some examples:

> I've never had any reason to be concerned about Merck.
> —Mozelle Faircloth, director of a nearby day care center

> I worked down there at Merck for 3 or 4 years. . . . Merck's a good company to be close to.
> —James Donaldson, 36-year resident of the area next to the plant

> They [Merck] are environmentally conscious and have a good record.
> —Scott Robertson, a compliance officer with the Georgia's Environmental Protection Department's hazardous waste unit

Few would disagree that Merck and Shell are admired companies. They are well managed, efficient, and financially very successful. Why the difference? Is it a matter of scale? Is it just a matter of chance? Is Merck lucky? Could Shell have avoided the problems it encountered?

It certainly could have—which is the message of this book. The public environment in which companies operate today, not just in the United States but worldwide, is far different than it was just 20 years ago. There are dramatic and far-reaching changes in the expectations of communities and societies today that define and influence how a company can operate. "Companies," cautions Gary Greve, president of BP Chemicals, "ignore community expectations at their own peril."[1]

Companies, therefore, that do not balance strategic intent with community expectations are likely to find their business aims and opportunities thwarted and, even more damaging, discover that their license to operate becomes increasingly curtailed. And the more a company's license to operate is curtailed, the more its ability to achieve a competitive advantage decreases.

At the same time, the public's changed expectations present significant economic opportunities for companies. Those that are positioned favorably in the community are treated differentially and respectfully. Time and expense needed to obtain permits are shorter and cheaper. Mistakes that happen are given the benefit of the doubt. Consumers are attracted to a company that promotes its good works. Employees prefer to work for companies that have a positive community reputation. In other words, what a company does in a community and how it does it can serve as a competitive advantage in the marketplace.

A successful company today, therefore, should pursue two goals, one necessary and the other optional.

1. It must redesign its community and operational practices in ways that respond to the community's expectations that increasingly now define how a company should operate.

2. It should take advantage of the public's shift in attitudes and design its community involvement programs to support its business goals and enhance its competitive advantage.

That is what this book is about. It proposes strategies based on the principle that companies need to be positioned in communities as desirable, trusted, and respected assets—or, in other words, to be what I call "a neighbor of choice." This is a necessary requirement to maintain the company's license to operate.

It also describes community relations strategies and programs that can both improve its community reputation and contribute to adding value to the company's economic goals. This is a good and sufficient reason to rethink the purpose of a company's community relations programs.

BACKGROUND

The development of the neighbor of choice principle and its strategies is based on my work over the past fifteen years teaching, consulting, and doing research in corporate community relations. As founder and now director emeritus of The Boston College Center for Corporate Community Relations, I have worked with over a thousand corporations around the world, helping them plan and develop community relations strategies and programs. This has been a rich source of information and experience, much of which forms the basis for the neighbor of choice principle and its strategies. Many of the examples used in the book come directly from my consulting with these companies.

The book is also based on my research and teaching of community planning in graduate schools for the past 30 years, along with my professional work in community planning for United Way and other community planning agencies. I cite these experiences deliberately. When a company engages in working with community leaders to develop positive relationships or contributes to the support of community organizations and agencies, it is intervening in the life of a community. Much like a community planning organization, the company is advocating for a point of view. The company wants its opinions and its contributions to be considered fairly and honestly.

To be successful in planning its community practices and programs, a company needs to understand how a community makes decisions and who gets involved and why they get involved in making or influencing community decisions. It also needs to be sensitive to the unique culture and values of the community in which it operates. The experience and practice of community planners, particularly those engaged in community planning in the voluntary sector, therefore, is a very useful background for understanding and guiding the community relations practices of companies.

A FEW WORDS ABOUT TERMINOLOGY

There are many different terms and points of view to describe the relationship between companies and communities. *Corporate social responsibility, corporate citizenship, corporate social responsiveness, government or public affairs, corporate social performance, corporate community affairs, corporate community investment,* and *corporate community relations* are some of the most common examples. There are a number of well-written and well-researched articles and books that describe each of these terms in detail.[2]

I prefer to use the term *community relations.* It is an expression commonly used by companies around the world to describe their community involvement activities and programs. It is also the term given to managers responsible for the company's community activities and programs.

Of equal importance, this is not a book about corporate philanthropy, although methods for designing contributions programs will be described. Neither is it about employee volunteerism, although corporate volunteer programs will be profiled. Nor is it about partnership programs with community organizations and schools. Success stories about partnerships as well as lessons learned from corporate experience will be described. This book is about the actions—total actions—of a company in the community and how a company goes about ensuring that its actions, as well as its community involvement programs, position it favorably in the community.

Community relations as it will be used in this book, therefore, is the state of relations between the company and the communities in which it has a presence or impact. It encompasses programs that advance the interests of both the company and its communities, such as donations, employee volunteerism, and community partnerships. It involves the impact of the operational activities of the company on its communities as well as programs established to develop relationships with groups and organizations in communities.[3]

While this book is about *corporate* community relations and the examples used to describe methods and techniques of community relations are derived from corporate experiences, many of the principles described can be applied to other types of organizations, such as colleges, universities, nonprofit organizations, and government agencies. The erosion of confidence, for example, in education is due in part to school districts' refusal to involve citizens and groups in their aims and planning. The unwillingness to involve communities in their deliberations has made governments the followers of community and societal expectations, not the promoters. Universities, similar to corporations, have been frustrated in achieving their planning goals.

Fordham University, for example, has had difficulty expanding a radio tower on its campus because of the opposition of its neighbor, the New York Botanical Gardens. Neighborhood groups have prevented Boston College from building a new teaching and student facility in the center of its campus, causing lengthy litigation and expensive construction delays. The Massachusetts Institute of

Technology (MIT) was required to fund a homeless organization in exchange for permission to expand one of its buildings. The 92nd Street Y in New York City wants to expand its facility to build additional classrooms on a vacant lot. The neighborhood has protested, organized a committee (Friends of Historic 92nd Street), and hired a lawyer to fight the Y's plan.

No organization, in other words, is immune from the changing forces and expectations of societies. Communities want to be involved in the planning and decisions of all organizations, not just corporations. Remaining indifferent or aloof from the community is an expensive folly.

ORGANIZATION OF THIS BOOK

Becoming a "neighbor of choice" describes the way a company has to be viewed to function in a changing public environment. It guides the development of the company's functional strategies, programs, and practices in the communities in which it operates.

Part I of the book outlines the forces that give rise to the need for adopting the neighbor of choice principle. Chapter 1 explains how communities have become increasingly important in influencing and defining a company's license or freedom to operate. It presents the concept of the psychological contract between companies and communities and how that contract has to be managed in order for a company to maintain its license to operate.

Chapter 2 describes the way a company has to respond to the changing psychological contract and the kinds of functional strategies that are needed to position the company as a neighbor of choice. It also provides a brief historical description of the evolution from an era of corporate philanthropy to the "neighbor of choice" solution as a guide for community relations practice.

A company cannot, for any length of time, engage in practices or activities that neglect its primary obligation to be competitive and successful in increasing shareholder value. Chapter 3 shows how the changes in attitudes and behaviors of customers and employees can be used to develop programs that help to sustain the competitive advantage of the company.

Part II of this book focuses on the implementation of the neighbor of choice principle. Chapter 4 describes the basic elements of the internal analysis needed in the formulation of strategies that take into consideration the company's business goals and objectives. Because of the complexity of the community environment, three chapters explain how to conduct an external or community environmental analysis. Chapter 5 describes the different kinds and types of communities in which a company operates. Chapter 6 describes the leadership patterns in communities and how to identify leaders and organizations that influence community decision making. Chapter 7 outlines the elements of the community assessment.

Part III describes the three strategies for becoming a neighbor of choice. A core strategy of the neighbor of choice principle is relationship building. Techniques for building sustainable relationships are described in Chapter 8. Chapter 9 describes the implementation of the second strategy, identifying and responding to the concerns and issues of the community. This chapter describes the kinds of relationship building and issues monitoring practices needed to respond to community concerns and to build trust in communities.

Chapters 10 and 11 focus on the third strategy of the neighbor of choice: a company's community programs. Chapter 10 describes the elements of a company's community programs and the role community programs have in building trust. Chapter 11 outlines how a company can use its community programs both to build trust and to achieve a competitive advantage.

Part IV explains the importance of a value or philosophical premise to achieving the full understanding of the neighbor of choice principle. Its sole chapter, Chapter 12, outlines the elements necessary for a company developing a social vision—the underlying premise of the neighbor of choice principle.

NOTES

1. G. Greve, "Global Neighbors: Commitment to Community Relations as a Key Business Strategy" (speech presented at the International Leaders Conference, 1998, Santa Barbara, March 16, 1998).

2. See, for example, C. L. Marsden and J. Andrio, "Towards an Understanding of Corporate Citizenship and How to Influence It," *Citizenship Studies Journal*, June 1998, pp. 329–352; D. J. Wood, "Corporate Social Performance Revisited," *Academy of Management Review*, Vol. 16, no. 4 (1991), pp. 661–718; D. J. Wood and P. L. Cochran, "Business and Society in Transition," *Business and Society*, Spring 1992, pp. 1–7; M. Sharfman, "Changing Institutional Rules," *Business and Society*, Vol. 33, no. 3 (December 1994), pp. 236–269; R. Ackerman and R. Bauer, *Corporate Social Responsiveness: The Modern Dilemma* (Reston, VA: Reston Publishing Company, 1976); C. Smith, "The New Corporate Philanthropy," *Harvard Business Review*, May–June 1994, pp. 105–116; R. E. Freeman and J. Liedtka, "Corporate Social Responsibility: A Critical Approach," *Business Horizons*, July–August 1991, pp. 92–98.

3. This is adapted from the definition of *community relations* used by The Center for Corporate Community Relations at Boston College. See "The Standards of Excellence in Community Relations: Guiding Principles for Community Relations Practice" (Boston: The Center for Corporate Community Relations at Boston College, 1994).

Part I

The Principle of the
Neighbor of Choice

Chapter 1

The *Psychological* Contract

When Shell U.K. was forced to reverse its decision to sink a used oil rig in the North Atlantic, it was not the first time a company was prevented from carrying out its business plans. Increasingly communities throughout the world are forcing companies to change their long-planned business decisions.

The Walt Disney Company, for example, was stopped from opening a theme park in northern Virginia; Monsanto was denied permission to open a plant in Bowling Green, Kentucky; Wal-Mart has been halted in efforts to open stores in Massachusetts, Vermont, and Virginia; in 1995 Calvin Klein had to withdraw its child jeans advertisements because they offended community sensibilities; the San Diego Chargers football team was held up in its plans to expand its new stadium; McDonald's, despite the active support of the prime minister, has been unable to open a restaurant in Bermuda; Battelle Institute was prevented from building a hazardous waste incinerator near its facility in Columbus, Ohio; the New England Patriots had to abandon plans to build a football stadium in Boston; environmental groups have forced du Pont to retreat from its plans to mine titanium in southeast Georgia; and a retired couple in Naples, Florida, organized residents to force U.S. Home Corporation, one of the nation's largest home builders, to withdraw its zoning request to build 45 residential units on land it had purchased. The list is never ending.

Why? What is stopping companies from pursuing their business goals and strategies—business goals and strategies that once went largely unquestioned?

Two reasons. First, the *psychological* contract—the implicit expectations that companies and communities have for each other—has changed. This change has gone unrecognized by many companies, and as a consequence, companies are making decisions based on incomplete information. The result is that they are reacting to events and circumstances, not shaping or defining them.

Second, the definer or who determines a company's license or freedom to operate has changed. Over the past 30 years the license to operate has shifted from the world's capitals to communities and neighborhoods. While most companies have begun to come to grips with this change and are marketing their community relations activities and hiring more staff, they still rely on programs that are out of date and often counterproductive. Nor do the programs they develop take full advantage of reducing costs or contributing to the company's competitive advantage.

THE PSYCHOLOGICAL CONTRACT

The psychological contract, unlike a social contract, which is explicit, contains both the explicit and unwritten expectations that companies and communities have for each other. It remains beneath the surface of relationships and is dynamic in character, continually changing, and frequently unacknowledged. It is a manifestation, too, of the ideals—ego ideals—that one party to the contract has for the other.

Developed by Harry Levinson, a leading management consultant on executive leadership and a former faculty member and now professor emeritus of the Harvard Business School, the psychological contract was formulated as a way to understand how to supervise and manage employees. Employees, specifically managers, according to Levinson, are attracted to companies based on their own values and needs.[1] They form bonds with companies and develop expectations of how the company should behave toward them. The company fosters these expectations by the attitudes it takes toward its employees, the benefits and services it provides, and the ethics, values, and ideologies the company upholds.

When managers join a company, they bring with them a number of specific needs, some of which are met and described in the job description. Others are not. These include the managers' hopes, aspirations, and ideals. Others are related to how managers want to be treated. They want to be treated with honesty, trust, and fairness. Managers want the opportunity to advance, even to believe that one day they could become chief executive officers (CEOs). In addition, they want to advance their skills and knowledge, form collegial relationships with other managers, and above all, be treated with respect and dignity.

The company, too, has both written and unwritten expectations for its managers. The explicit expectations are contained in job descriptions of its policies, benefit plans, and department or company mission statements and are discussed in performance reviews. The implied expectations include loyalty, trustworthiness, and dependable work habits. A company also expects its managers to go beyond the job description in crises or emergencies, not to embarrass or scandalize the company, keep the company's secrets, respect confidentiality, support and protect colleagues, and work pleasantly and cooperatively in teams.

These combined expectations form the psychological contract. Although it is unwritten, each party tacitly assumes that such a contract exists, and each expects the other to act in keeping it. "When," claims Levinson, "one or another party to the contract unilaterally violates it, then the other reacts with all the anger and frustration that usually follows an experience of being treated unfairly."[2]

THE PSYCHOLOGICAL CONTRACT BETWEEN COMPANIES AND COMMUNITIES

There is a remarkable and instructive similarity between the psychological contract companies have with managers and those they have with communities. Just as employees have expectations for a company that reflect their ego ideals of how they should be treated, so, too, do communities have ego ideals of how the company should treat the community. Communities represent more than a place to live, work, shop, and do business. They provide an intangible and psychological bond that knit people together.

People want to live in communities that are clean, environmentally safe, friendly, and cooperative. It is the place to raise families, to grow businesses, and to prosper and survive. People work together to achieve these ends that are shared in common. While these are aspirations and may not be fully achievable, there is the expectation that everyone is seeking to achieve them in common. There is a reciprocity of trust—a common basis, a common set of values, that joins people together to live the good life. It is the implicit expectations that communities and companies have for each other. There are recognized values that are held in common—a company needs to remain competitive and a community needs to be treated honestly and fairly—and there will be a mutual attempt to make each other successful in achieving these ends.

It is surprising to some to hear about individuals who turn down opportunities to move to other communities to advance their job or to be near family members when they grow old. A recent article in the *New York Times* about the growing number of elderly who remain in rural communities catches the essence of what communities mean to people.

"My neighbor just got back from visiting her family for a month in California," said one resident. "She said she didn't realize how much it meant to be in a small town where everybody knows you and you know everybody."

"I know what it means. When I walk down the street, people call me by my name."

"It also means that after years of paying into the small town-version of Social Security—volunteering at church, shopping on Main Street, cooking for the sick, being a good neighbor, people can count on people looking out for each other."

"You got somebody in your neighborhood who's older, needs help, we do it," said one 75 year old community resident.[3]

Communities, in other words, have deep meanings for people. People long for their communities to retain the values that have sustained them. This is the ideal that people hold out for communities and the basis for anger and resentment when those ideals are violated by companies. The contract—the psychological contract—has been destroyed.

Many social theorists describe what they call the loss of community. "They express," claim two professors of city planning at Ohio State University, "nostalgia for the interdependence of small town life, rural life or the Greek polis. They blame industrialization, large-scale bureaucracies, the loss of local autonomy, and our culture of mobility, convenience, and privacy for the decline in the sense of community."[4]

Levinson describes the example of the American Oil Company closing an obsolete refinery in Neodesha, Kansas. "A year before they did so," Levinson writes,

they sent an executive to the community and plant who announced the projected closing. Each employee was interviewed for possible transfer to another refinery or to ascertain his skills for other local jobs. Other companies were solicited for possible job openings. The refinery site was turned over to the community for an industrial park. The company helped the community find other industries for the park. When the change was completed, over 300 people were employed where 200 had been before and everyone working together had been able to adapt to the change successfully. The company wasn't being altogether charitable. It had closed another refinery in Louisiana earlier without doing something like this and had felt the repercussions through the influence of that state's senator. When a company is concerned about perpetuation, it soon learns that it cannot do with short-term expedient solutions.[5]

The expectations that companies and communities have for each other may be different in character than those between managers and companies. They are, nonetheless, real. Some are explicit: pay taxes, obey the laws and ordinances in the community, and provide employment opportunities for the residents. At the same time, companies have specific expectations of communities. They expect that communities will provide the infrastructure for the companies' operations—police, fire protection, and transportation facilities, for example. They also expect an educated workforce.

The implicit expectations focus on the intangible and are often part of the values, hopes, and ideals the company or the community has for itself, and these are in continual flux. It is very enlightening to see how the expectations companies and communities have for each other have changed over the years.

In the executive education programs I conduct, executives are asked to identify unwritten expectations over two periods: expectations 30 years ago and those that are current. In doing so, I use four questions to guide the answers.

What does the community want from the company?
How does the community expect the company to behave or act?

What does the community want the company to stand for?
What wouldn't the community want the company to do?

Similar questions are asked about the company.

What does the company want from the community?
How does the company expect the community to behave or act toward it?
What wouldn't the company want the community to do?

This is a sample of answers combined from recent programs:

Community expectations in the past:
Provide lifetime employment to residents
Contribute money and leadership to major charities (almost exclusively 30 years ago, United Way, local hospital, community museum)
Provide leadership to important community projects
Support the community's values and way of life
Be moral and ethical in dealings with employees, consumers, and the community
Encourage executives to take an active part in a church
Be involved in civic and business organizations

Company expectations in the past:
Educate a workforce with responsible and dependable work habits (''Keep your nose clean and get to work on time,'' the advice one manager reported she was given by her father)
Trust that the company's decisions, both for the company and the community, are in the best interests of the community
Loyalty to the company
Buy products of the community's companies
Support company's community interests and projects
Be proud of company and its employees

Community expectations in the present:
Provide employment opportunities (no longer necessarily lifetime)
Be environmentally responsible
Correct past environmental mistakes and problems
Keep community informed about current and future business plans and involve community representatives in those decisions that can have an impact on the community
Understand and respond to the concerns and interests of the community
Contribute to community charities and to the support of public agencies
Be involved as a partner and as a financial contributor to improving public education

Loan executives to community agencies

Encourage and support employee volunteer programs

Take the lead in solving community problems

Company expectations in the present:

Educate a workforce that can meet the company's growing technological needs

Support the company's freedom to operate

Provide social services needed to maintain a workforce (day care services for children, for example)

Trust that the company's decisions are in the best interests of the community

Loyalty

Support company's community interests and projects

Be proud of company and its employees

Reduce crime and delinquency

Understand the company's business problems, particularly the growing globally competitive environment under which companies now operate

Not only have the number and substance of the expectations that companies and communities have for each other changed over time, but there are some obvious conflicts. Executives tell me that there is a growing distrust of their companies. Communities believe companies are no longer interested in their well-being or even concerned about their survival. Yet companies expect loyalty.

These observations are not at all too different than what others have found. In a weeklong series in the *New York Times*, for example, reporters described the impact of downsizing on the country.[6] Excerpts from the series are instructive:

Describing the results of AT&T's hostile takeover of the National Cash Register Company (NCR) in Dayton, Ohio, a local banker, George Bayless, says, "NCR was part of Dayton's soul."

Another observation: "The Cash got rich selling its cash registers to the world, and it rewarded its workers with good livings and unrivaled benefits, and its hometown with a firm hand of civic guidance and millions of dollars of good works. They were all bound together—the company, the workers, and the town. To a lot of people here, Dayton was the Cash, and the Cash was Dayton."

Describing a speech the new executive of the AT&T's acquisition made to a luncheon meeting of business and community leaders, Frederick C. Smith, the retired chief executive of Dayton-based Huffy Bicycle, told his wife:

Figure 1.1
The Psychological Contract

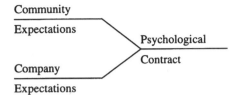

Source: Adapted and used with the permission of the Levinson Institute.

"He talked for one hour, almost non stop, and left precisely at 1 o'clock. I didn't understand a word he said. It was all about the information highway and globalization and, 'It's a new world.' [He] didn't know a thing about Dayton."

Trust, the shared vision of what people in communities have for companies, has changed significantly. For that reason, communities, through their representatives or as part of organized groups, are forcing companies to display new forms of responsibility and citizenship to their communities.

Company expectations have also changed. Companies, too, feel that they are not understood. Communities are insensitive to the ever increasing competitiveness of the global economy. Communities refuse to help companies implement programs that will help them remain competitive. In fact, communities seem intent on burdening companies with regulatory requirements that only increase costs and reduce a company's ability to compete. The loyalty that communities had for companies no longer exists.

The combination of these expectations forms the psychological contract (see Figure 1.1). It is not uncommon for these expectations to go unrecognized for years. Communities and companies may not even be aware of them. Or they may be a nuisance, a minor irritant that lies beneath the surface of the relationships.

But when a significant change occurs, the conflict in expectations becomes readily apparent and ripe for causing problems. The company may announce an expansion, a new manufacturing process that has environmental implications, or a decrease in support of community institutions. It may be discovered that the company has been leaking chemicals into a local river. A fire or chemical spill may occur. Or the company may announce it is moving.

Communities, too, make decisions based on their own expectations, which can conflict with company expectations. A community may introduce regulations governing business processes or plans. It may bring a company to court for backing out of a promise to maintain employment levels in return for tax relief. It may call for increased enforcement and penalties for manufacturing accidents. It may publicly criticize or embarrass a company or call for a boycott of its products such as the much publicized boycotts of Coors, Nike, Liz Claiborne, and Denny's Restaurants.

When such significant changes take place the psychological contract is violated, whether a violation was intended or not. If there is no strategy or plan in place for managing the expectations, conflict is likely to erupt. The tendency on the part of the company is to feel betrayed. Frequently, a company acts defensively. Michael Eisner's defense of the Disney Company's theme park in northern Virginia is a classic illustration. In a letter to the *New York Times*, Eisner, chairman and CEO, said, "American students do not know enough about American history. We have always been concerned to help educate through entertainment. We plan to . . . build a park that will do something that has never been done before." He also wrote, "We have not complained about the 33 local, state, and federal hurdles and the need to get 72 permits."[7] Eisner was hurt. The company's intentions were noble. He was building an educational venture that would create 12,000 new jobs, generate $1.68 billion in taxes, build new roads, and comply with all regulatory requirements. But he was spurned.

Eisner's response is not unusual. Similar claims are made by other companies that are trying to expand or maintain existing operations and manufacturing processes. They, too, insist that their intentions are honorable and will bring untold benefits to the community. They often publicize the company's generosity, all it has done for the community in the past. They employ lobbyists to influence legislators—but frequently to no avail or to frustrating and costly delays. And with each contention, the license to operate becomes narrower and narrower.

The lessons of employee relationships in the past are instructive. Just as companies learned how to manage the psychological contract—the changing expectations—between managers and the company, they now need to apply that learning to manage the contract between the company and the community.

The psychological contract can be renegotiated. But it can only be renegotiated in an environment of trust. And it can only be renegotiated after a relationship is established between the company and the community—a point I will return to and explain in later chapters.

THE COMMUNITY AS THE DEFINER OF THE LICENSE TO OPERATE

The license to operate is a preeminent right. It is, as Cor Herkstroter, chairman of the Committee of Managing Directors of Royal Dutch Shell, says, "the activities which societies allow a [company] to undertake as a private, profit making enterprise."[8] A company's license to operate, in other words, defines what it can and cannot do.

For a great many years the license to operate has been determined largely by federal or national governments. In the United States it was the federal government. It established laws and regulations to govern many facets of a company's business, including wages, prices, health, safety, environment, and pensions. Even more important, Washington set the domestic policy agenda, which had significant implications for business. During the Eisenhower years it was the highway program and urban renewal. In the Kennedy/Johnson era it was community mental health, welfare reform, civil rights, elderly pensions, the Peace Corps, Model Cities, VISTA, and citizen participation.

Understandably, corporations developed external affairs strategies aimed at influencing legislation and the government regulatory process. It is significant to note that the Public Affairs Council, an association of corporate government relations and public affairs officials located in Washington, D.C., was established in 1954 to coordinate these efforts. The Council, interestingly enough, was formed at the suggestion of President Dwight Eisenhower, who urged business leaders to become involved in politics and government.

The domestic policy agenda however, is no longer defined in Washington or in the capitals of most democratic nations. In the United States, for example, with the exception of taxes, every major domestic policy program since the early 1960s has been set, shaped, and in some cases designed by organizations and citizen advocacy groups. The agendas defining highway safety, environmental practices, disability access, work and family accommodations, and AIDS (acquired immunodeficiency syndrome) research, for example, have come from the organized efforts of advocacy groups. And in each instance, the legislation that has emerged has had economic consequences for business.

Environment is a classic illustration. Nearly all the environmental policy beginning with the 1962 publication of Rachel Carson's book *Silent Spring* has been initiated and defined by a myriad of environmental organizations and coalitions. The Clean Air Act, The Emergency Planning and Community Right-to-Know Act, Title III of the Superfund Amendments and Reauthorization Act of 1986, and the Endangered Species Act are a few examples. The continuing debates on electromagnetic fields and the safety of computer monitors are others.

The federal laws covering the drinking age for minors constitute another example. The killing by a drunk driver of a young girl in Los Angeles persuaded a mother, Candy Lightner, to protest the ''slap on the wrist'' judgment that was customary at that time. She organized other mothers, first in Los Angeles, then across the country, who had suffered similar child deaths. Her inspiration and efforts led to the national organization Mothers against Drunk Driving (MADD), which has successfully influenced legislators, judges, and even more significantly, the general public to change their attitudes about the dangers of drinking and driving.

MADD was also successful in forcing President Ronald Reagan to sign legislation to which he was adamantly opposed. Included in the Highway Safety reauthorization bill was an amendment proposed by MADD to raise the drinking age in all states to 21. Reagan was ready to veto the legislation because he believed that this was a state's rights issue. His staff persuaded him, however, to sign the bill rather than risk the enmity of parents throughout the country.

The influence that community and advocacy groups have over defining the social policy agenda is not confined to the United States. Community and advocacy groups influence the world's policy agenda. Environment is a common example. The demands for companies to be environmentally responsible is common in all societies and even growing in Third World countries. But there are other examples.

In late 1961 a group of political activists who had been active in campaigns against the Vietnam War were meeting in Washington, D.C., to discuss new campaigns. They began a discussion about victims of land mines. Some had been active in providing prosthetics for land mine victims in Central America. (Incidentally, this is an example of a so-called iron law of organizations. Once they have completed their agenda, community organizations customarily do not go out of business but look for other issues to organize around. The association itself provides satisfactions over and above the purpose and mission of the organization, which is enough of an incentive to keep the organization alive.)[9] The group established the International Committee to Ban Landmines, which persuaded over 100 nations to sign a treaty outlawing the use of land mines. The organization subsequently was awarded the 1997 Nobel Peace Prize for its efforts. As the *New York Times* reported: "The story of how a tiny but determined band of outsiders took on and defeated some of the world's great powers at their own game—diplomacy—says a lot about the increasing role of public pressure in world affairs."[10]

Advocacy and community groups not only are influential in setting the agenda; they also monitor corporate performance. In Cincinnati, for example, a neighborhood group won a $78 million settlement against a uranium processing plant. The Association of Community Organizations for Reform Now (ACORN) accused Allstate Insurance Co. of "blatantly violating fair housing and insurance laws" in seventeen cities. The National Committee for Responsive Philanthropy has mobilized alternative fund organizations to confront major telephone organizations about their giving practices to racial and ethnic populations. AIDS organizations have closed down the New York Stock Exchange to protest the high price of AIDS medicine. Advocates for the disabled rolled their wheelchairs in front of Greyhound buses, disrupting business in New York City, because of the lack of access for the disabled to the large interstate bus companies. In Boston, Fleet Financial Group was forced to contribute $20 million for inner-city loans because of lending violations uncovered and publicized by neighborhood advocates for subsidized housing.

The community has emerged as the place where the policy agenda is defined and implemented. *Community control,* consequently, has become a watchword for neighborhood activists, mayors, governors, and public policy experts. Decentralization of federal programs begun under the Reagan administration is now called *reinventing government* by the Clinton administration. Borrowed from the works of policy experts David Osborne and Ted Gaebler, the reinventing government focus is to empower states and communities to control their own destinies.[11]

The elections in 1996 further hardened the shift of power from the federal to

[handwritten: Community as major stakeholder]

local governments. The national capital has become powerless through gridlock and inaction. Gun control legislation, for example, has moved from Washington to the state legislatures. And the Supreme Court has become an ally of the states, overturning federal regulations and upholding state laws. While Congress thrashed about trying to pass legislation on tobacco, by the summer of 1998 41 states had passed their own tobacco laws. Thad L. Beyle, a political science professor at the University of North Carolina quoted in the *New York Times*, warns, "the states are getting to be where a lot of the action is. And it will continue that way until we have a major depression or other catastrophe."[12]

It is the community, consequently, that has emerged since the 1970s as a significant stakeholder determining a company's license to operate.[13] As Richard Evans, vice president of Amoco Corp., explained, "Companies operate only with the permission of the community. And that permission," he added, "has to be earned."[14] Companies unable to understand this shift repeatedly run into trouble, frequently with painful and costly consequences.

Obviously, of course, it is not communities that have stakeholder relationships with companies but individuals and groups in communities. Some have legitimate authority for defining the company's license to operate, such as elected and appointed public officials. Others, such as activist groups, using a variety of techniques and tactics, can use influence with public officials to define how, when, and where a company can operate.[15] How this is accomplished will be described in later chapters.

To stay in business, therefore, to preserve its license to operate, a company has to put in place *corporate* strategies that take into account the new role of communities in defining the policy and regulatory agendas.

SUMMARY

Since the beginning of the 1970s, attitudes, expectations, and behaviors toward companies have shifted dramatically. These changes have had an enormous impact on all companies' license to operate. The freedom that companies once had for making business decisions has become constrained. Attitudes, expectations, and behavior in communities, consequently, have to be managed, as any other function in the company has to be managed. If they are not, companies will see their license to operate continue to erode and their competitive strategies become unworkable.

The shift in the center of government and regulatory influence of companies has also changed. The community has become the focal point for decision making that affects companies. As former Speaker of the U.S. House of Representatives Thomas "Tip" O'Neill commented, "All politics is local." Consequently, any company's external affairs strategy has to take into account these two new realities:

1. The expectations that communities and companies have for each other—or what I have termed the psychological contract—have changed and will continue to change.

2. The community, not the federal government, has become the major influence in defining or determining a company's license to operate.

In the next chapter, we will examine how these changes have affected the community relations programs and practices of companies.

NOTES

1. See H. Levinson, *Psychological Man* (Cambridge, MA: The Levinson Institute, 1976), pp. 90–91.

2. Ibid., p. 91.

3. S. Rimer, "Rural Elderly Create Vital Communities as Young Leave Void," *New York Times*, February 2, 1998, p. A14.

4. J. L. Nasar and D. A. Julian, "The Psychological Sense of Community in the Neighborhood," *APA Journal*, Spring 1995, p. 178.

5. Levinson, *Psychological Man*, p. 93.

6. "A Hometown Feels Less Like Home: The Downsizing of America," *New York Times*, March 6, 1996, pp. A1, A16–A17.

7. M. Eisner, Letter to the Editor, *New York Times*, June 23, 1994.

8. C. Herkstroter, "Shell's License to Operate," *Corporate Public Affairs*, Vol. 6, no. 4 (1996), pp. 10–16.

9. Columbia University, Bureau of Applied Social Research, *The Volunteers: Means and Ends in a National Organization*, a report by David L. Sill (Glencoe, IL: Free Press, 1957).

10. R. Bonner, "How a Group of Outsiders Moved Nations to Ban Land Mines," *New York Times*, September 20, 1997, p. 5.

11. D. Osborne and T. Gaebler, *Reinventing Government: How the Entrepreneurial Spirit Is Transforming the Public Sector* (Reading, MA: Addison-Wesley, 1992).

12. R. L. Berke, "Social Issues Shift to States," *New York Times*, October 19, 1997, sec. 4, p. 5.

13. This is based on Freeman's broad definition of *stakeholder theory*. R. E. Freeman, *Strategic Management: A Stakeholder Approach* (Boston: Pitman, 1984).

14. R. E. Evans, "Community Relations: The Key to Operations Success" (speech presented at the 1993 Community Relations Leaders Conference sponsored by the Center for Corporate Community Relations at Boston College, Chicago, 1993).

15. See R. K. Mitchell, B. R. Agle, and D. J. Wood, "Toward a Theory of Stakeholder Identification and Salience: Defining the Principle of Who Counts and What Really Counts," *Academy of Management Review*, Vol. 22, no. 4 (1997), pp. 853–886.

Chapter 2

From Balloons and T-Shirts
to Neighbor of Choice

Prior to the 1980s, a company's contributions programs consisted solely of charitable contributions. It was a small, grudgingly accepted program by corporate officials that was limited to high-profile charities. Often referred to as the "balloons and T-shirts" era by community relations managers, community relations was defined almost exclusively as giving grants to noncontroversial nonprofit organizations— hospital, museum, United Way, and frequently the CEO's alma mater. Contributions decisions were made by the CEO in response to pressures from other CEOs or influential community leaders, members of the board, and even in some instances, the CEO's spouse.

While this type of checkbook philanthropy has faded, there are still remnants of this practice by a few companies. When James Agee was CEO of Morris Knudsen Company in the 1990s, for example, he appointed his wife, Mary Cunningham, to chair the company's charitable foundation. She, in turn, selected wives of the company's board to serve on the foundation to award grants to their favorite charities. Cunningham angered members of the company's board because she directed charitable dollars to organizations providing alternatives to abortion.[1]

RESPONDING TO MANAGEMENT CHALLENGES

Beginning with the election of President Ronald Reagan in 1980, the course of corporate philanthropy began to shift markedly, changing from the stage of checkbook philanthropy to finding ways to manage a greatly expanding function that included not only charitable donations but also gifts of products and establishment of employee volunteer programs. Reagan introduced drastic cuts in social programs, amounting initially to over $11 billion. The nonprofit agencies were particularly hard hit. In the first year, 57 percent of the voluntary agencies experienced reductions in federal funds. The United Way reported that in 1981 one out of every five dollars cut from the federal budgets would affect nonprofit agencies.

At the same time, the president urged the business community to pick up the support for local charities. In a speech to the National Alliance of Business, he challenged the business community to become involved in alleviating social problems. He issued an executive order to form a 44-member task force headed by C. William Verity, at that time chairman of Armco, Inc., "to support and promote private sector leadership and responsibility for meeting public needs . . . and to serve as a focal point for private sector action addressing public programs."[2] The president also asked corporations to double their philanthropic contributions. And he argued that volunteers and voluntary agencies could provide many of the needed social services that were presently being provided through federal dollars.

It was not only the corporations who heard the president's call to support community charities, it was also the charities. Consequently, corporations were besieged with requests for funds, loaned staff, and donations of equipment. Requests came not only from voluntary agencies but from an entirely new source of "charitable" organization—government agencies who were also faced with large-scale budget reductions.

Corporate contributions soared. Between 1976 and 1985, corporate gifts to charity tripled, rising from about $1.5 billion to $4.4. billion. Since 1990, corporate contributions have continued to increase but at a slower rate. The increases have not kept pace with inflation. In 1996, corporate contributions to charity amounted to $8.5 billion. (This figure itself is questionable, as I will explain in Chapter 4.) Corporate contributions represented 5.6 percent of total charitable contributions from all sources (individual, foundation, and bequests). Since 1995, corporate contributions have remained steady at 1.3 percent of pretax income.[3]

However dramatic the increases in funding, they did not in any way equal the cuts in funding to human and social service programs. The Reagan budgets, it was estimated, reduced federal programs by $33 billion. There was no way, a report from the American Association of Fund-Raising Council warned, that corporations were going to make up the $33 billion that Reagan was cutting from the federal budget.[4]

At the same time the number of nonprofit organizations began to grow exponentially. Between 1977 and 1994 the number of nonprofits increased from 739,000 to over a million. Some 5.5 million people were employed in nonprofit organizations in 1977. By 1994 that number had almost doubled to over 9.5 million employees. The nonprofit sector grew faster than government or business, fueling an ever increasing demand for corporate help. Reagan unwittingly had redefined the psychological contract.

Corporations found themselves overwhelmed. CEOs were becoming besieged with requests for donations in the mail, on the phone, and at meetings and even social gatherings. They could not keep up with the demand. Nor could they keep increasing contributions. Companies were forced to reshape and change their practices. Staff was recruited or staff was borrowed from other departments, such as communications and public relations, to take charge.

The staffs, in turn, sought assistance in learning how to manage a rapidly growing function. The Public Affairs Council, a Washington-based organization of public and government affairs officials, organized a conference for community relations managers in Minneapolis in 1984. A few years later they organized a conference on strategic philanthropy.

The Boston College Center for Corporate Community Relations was started in 1985 to respond to the professional development and research needs of the emerging corporate community relations managers. The knowledge base for the practice of community relations expanded from understanding the legal and practical aspects of grant making to the politics of community decision making, issues analysis, working with advocacy groups, and managing an ever growing function. The Center's Standards of Excellence are widely accepted as the norm for excellence in community relations practice.

VOLUNTEER, The National Organization, which was established to promote volunteerism, helped establish employee volunteer centers in major cities throughout the country. Many were organized as part of local United Way agencies. VOLUNTEER has since been merged with the Points of Light Foundation (POLF). POLF, an organization started by President George Bush, has engaged in a national and well publicized effort to promote employee volunteerism. Its annual awards program to the best employee volunteer program is eagerly sought after by major corporations. A study it conducted in collaboration with the Conference Board, a business research organization, describes the positive impact of volunteerism on employee morale and professional development.

In the United Kingdom the Prince of Wales founded an organization called Business in the Community (BITC) to support corporate involvement in community affairs. BITC operates community ventures, such as training programs for the unemployed in partnerships with corporations. Prince Charles became a strong advocate for corporate community involvement because he believed it would not only help local communities but also enable U.K. companies to increase their competitive advantage in the European Common Market. Most large corporations in the United Kingdom supported the prince's ideas and efforts. "Community educational programmes are based on the needs of our business," said Chris Marsden, former head of community relations for the British Petroleum Co., "not altruism."[5]

In Tokyo, the Keidanren (Japan Federation of Economic Organizations), the principal organization of major Japanese corporations, set up the Council for Better Corporate Citizenship in 1989 to promote corporate philanthropy. It urged Japanese corporations to contribute 1 percent of their profits to philanthropy. "Philanthropy," said Gaishi Hiraiwa, Keidanren chairman, "should be set in place as the 'fourth pillar' of managment following customers, shareholders and employees."[6]

One of the earliest organizations was Philippine Business for Social Progress. It was started in 1970 by 50 leading Philippine corporations. The initial focus was to design community programs to address poverty in the country. Philippine Business for Social Progress has close to 200 corporate members and has helped initiate community projects to improve the quality of community life in the Philippines. Philippine Business for Social Progress also conducts training programs for major companies in Southeast Asia.

The Centre for Corporate Public Affairs in Australia is another business-led organization devoted to community affairs in Australia and New Zealand. It publishes a newsletter, provides consultation, and conducts training programs for corporate managers.

During this period, corporations began to redefine *their* expectations for the community. The need for a technologically prepared workforce became increasingly important as the knowledge economy and global competition emerged. Public schools, American industry discovered, were not able to keep pace with these changes. Corporate involvement in public schools became a community relations priority. "In case after case," says Louis V. Gerstner, Jr., chairman and CEO of IBM, "American Industry has discovered that the skills of the past are not even marginally adequate for the present. When Motorola decided to 'make it in America' they had not only to retrain but to reeducate many members of their workforce."[7]

In addition, the changing character of the workforce—two wage-earner parents, single-parent families, the sandwich generation—revealed glaring human services needs for companies that companies were unable to offer. Some, such as IBM, set up child care and elder care referral services for their employees. Others like AT&T gave direct contributions to child care agencies. The AT&T program was part of a labor management agreement.[8]

It was becoming increasingly evident that there was a very direct connection between a company's business aims and its community programs. But even more evidence of what companies began calling the "business case" for corporate philanthropy began to emerge in the late 1980s.

COMMUNITY INVOLVEMENT AS A COMPETITIVE EDGE

During the latter part of the 1980s, a spate of reports from opinion research and advertising agencies began to emerge, ushering in a third stage in the development of corporate community relations practices. Consumers, said one group of studies, were more likely to buy products from companies that had a good community record than from ones that did not, thereby providing companies with a "competitive edge." Surveys conducted by advertising and marketing companies, such as the Wirthlin Group, Grey Advertising, Walker Research, and Cone Communications in the United States and Market Opinion

Research International in London, revealed that consumers are influenced by a company's community reputation.[9] This is a reflection of what marketing experts call the "new age consumer"—consumers who, according to Grey Advertising, are fearful of an uncertain economy and therefore interested in value, accountability, trust, and *corporate responsibility.*

The attitude shift also spawned advocacy organizations promoting corporate social responsibility to consumers. The Council for Economic Priorities, for example, sold over 850,000 copies of *Shopping for a Better World*, which rates the makers of over 1,800 brand-name products on eleven issues, including community relations and philanthropy.

Moreover, consumer and environmental organizations appealed to consumers to get their messages across. Environmental organizations forced H. J. Heinz to agree that it would not buy tuna from companies that used nets. Rainforest Action Network asks consumers to boycott Mitsubishi products on the basis that one of its companies harvests wood in the rainforests. The National Association for the Advancement of Colored People (NAACP) monitors affirmative action programs of major corporations and in fact has negotiated agreements to increase black employment with several major corporations, including a $1 billion settlement with Denny's restaurant chain. Former NAACP director Rev. Benjamin F. Chavis, Jr., states the question bluntly: "Does it not make good business sense for companies to redefine their relationship with a multiracial society?"[10]

These reports were soon followed up by articles appearing in the academic press, lending a degree of authenticity to the claims of advertisers.[11] Furthermore, a shift in attitude among top managers emerged. Socially responsible corporate actions were felt by managers to have an effect on market share, which in turned influenced their decision making. A company's reputation in the community could provide a company a competitive advantage, reported an article in *Review of Business* by two researchers.[12]

CAUSE-RELATED MARKETING

This shift in consumer behavior gave rise to two marketing developments. One is "cause-related marketing," a term coined and copyrighted by the Travel Related Services unit of American Express Company. In 1983 American Express Company announced it would donate a penny for each use of its charge card and a dollar for each new card issued over a four-month period, with the money going to renovate the Statue of Liberty. The results surpassed expectations. The company had a 28 percent increase in card usage, compared with the same period in the previous year, and a significant increase in new cards issued. Close to $2 million was turned over to the Statue of Liberty—Ellis Island Foundation.[13]

The success of American Express Company's Statue of Liberty campaign, along with studies showing the many benefits of cause marketing, led many other companies to follow suit. One case study analysis indicated that cause marketing could achieve the following objectives:

Gain national visibility

Enhance corporate image

Thwart negative publicity

Pacify customer groups

Generate incremental sales

Promote repeat purchases

Promote multiple unit purchases

Increase brand awareness, recognition, and image

Reinforce brand image

Broaden customer base

Reach new market segments and geographic markets

Increase level of merchandising activity at the retail level for the brand[14]

"Cause marketing," reported two researchers, "may be the most creative and cost-effective product marketing strategy to evolve in years."[15] But it is fundamentally a marketing strategy.

The second philanthropic marketing strategy is called "social marketing" and is designed to influence consumers indirectly. Social marketing is aimed at persuading people to engage in socially responsible behavior, which may in turn rebound to the benefit of a company. For example, Eveready Battery Company launched a public education campaign in 1988 to encourage people to change batteries in smoke detectors once a year when clocks were turned back from daylight savings time. They recruited the International Association of Fire Chiefs to cosponsor the campaign. It was a huge success. It generated 1 billion media impressions equivalent to $20.9 million in advertising. The program was featured on major television and radio programs. And the promotion increased sales by 89 percent during its first year. Eveready was the beneficiary of most of the sales.

Other examples include Kellogg's campaign to tie in AllBran cereal with promotion of a high-fiber, low-fat diet in association with the National Cancer Institute. Avon sponsors a breast cancer awareness crusade. And Ryka, a manufacturer of women's athletic shoes, has promoted campaigns to end violence against women.[16]

Cause- and social-related marketing strategies are not without critics. Some nonprofits view such efforts, particularly cause-related marketing, as unethical and manipulative. It is viewed as weakening the nonprofit organization and "selling out" the nonprofit world, according to one study. The study reported nonprofit groups as saying that cause marketing unduly associated the nonprofit

organization with commercialism, set up obstacles to forging rapport with do-
nors, and compromised the nonprofit organization.[17]

Peter Goldberg, a former vice president of American Can Company, said that
cause marketing may prove advantageous for nonprofits that are "marketable."
But most agencies that serve clients with serious social problems, such as AIDS,
teen pregnancy, child abuse, and refugee settlement, may be left out.[18]

The National Committee for Responsive Philanthropy, an alternative organization to the United Way of America, has also voiced criticism to the business
case development of corporate giving programs. Only organizations that are
nonthreatening or noncontroversial, according to Robert Bothwell, the organization's executive director, will be supported. Many community needs will be
left wanting.[19]

As a consequence of the business- and marketing-focused strategies, the National Committee for Responsive Philanthropy launched a national effort in 1992
to urge corporations to direct their contributions to racial and ethnic minorities.
It conducted meetings with corporate executives, demanding that they explain
their grant-making priorities. The aim of the project "What Color Is Your Proposal?" is to force corporations to change grant-making priorities to include
organizations representing minorities and low-income families.

EMPLOYEE ATTITUDES TOWARD CORPORATE
COMMUNITY INVOLVEMENT

Employees, companies were discovering, were also influenced by a company's community image. A survey conducted by Research and Forecasts for
the Chivas Regal Company found that job loyalty is greater in companies that
are active in the community. Over half of the study's respondents also said that
if they knew the CEO volunteered time in the community, their loyalty to the
CEO and the company would increase. Surprisingly, less than half the employees knew anything about the company's community involvement.[20] Another interesting finding from *The Chivas Regal Report* that tends to reveal broader
implications about the values of today's workers is that more workers cited the
ability to do some good in the world (15 percent) than cited earning great wealth
(10 percent). Only a "happy family life" was chosen more often.[21]

A survey of human resource executives conducted by the Conference Board
(see Figure 2.1) revealed that a company's reputation in the community had a
major impact on a company's ability to be viewed as an employer of choice by
employees. Community reputation was ranked third out of 21 factors believed
to have a "great deal" of impact on employees choosing to join a company.
Only career development, chosen by 68 percent of the respondents, and a company's compensation plan, chosen by 65 percent, were ranked higher. Community reputation was chosen by 61 percent of the human resource respondents
as an important attribute for a company.[22]

Motorola, according to Patrick Canavan, corporate vice president and director,

Figure 2.1
Characteristics That Define an Employer of Choice

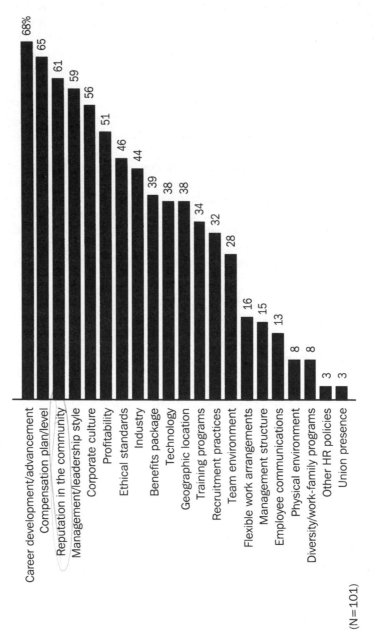

Characteristic	Percent
Career development/advancement	68%
Compensation plan/level	65
Reputation in the community	61
Management/leadership style	59
Corporate culture	56
Profitability	51
Ethical standards	46
Industry	44
Benefits package	39
Technology	38
Geographic location	38
Training programs	34
Recruitment practices	32
Team environment	28
Flexible work arrangements	16
Management structure	15
Employee communications	13
Physical environment	8
Diversity/work-family programs	8
Other HR policies	3
Union presence	3

(N=101)

Source: Conference Board, *H.R. Executive Review: Competing as an Employer of Choice* (New York: Conference Board, 1996), p. 4. Reprinted with the permission of the Conference Board.

Global Leadership and Organizational Development, speaking at the 1995 Community Relations Leaders Conference, uses its community relations programs as strategies for recruiting and maintaining a skilled workforce.[23]

William Safire, the *New York Times* columnist who is opposed to corporate social responsibility (he calls it "The New Socialism") admits, however, that "good community relations helps attract the best managers and innovators to a company."[24]

A more rigorous and theoretically based study examined the impact of a company's social performance on recruiting and retaining employees. Researchers at the University of Missouri found that a company's corporate social performance is "positively related to their reputations and attractiveness as an employer."[25] In an era when human resources is becoming the investment capital of the twenty-first century, findings such as these become even more significant.

In further shifts, companies began using community volunteer programs to achieve personal development objectives. Thom McAn and United Parcel Service (UPS) have used volunteer programs to help managers become sensitive to diversity issues.[26] General Electric uses volunteer programs to teach team building skills. And many companies encourage managers to take leadership roles in nonprofit organizations as a way to develop presentation, planning, and organizational skills.[27]

UPS developed an Urban Internship program for its mid- and senior managers as a significant part of their professional development. Each year the company sends 40 managers into four different internship programs run by nonprofit agencies. As of 1993, over 850 managers had participated as interns.

THE NEIGHBOR OF CHOICE

The fourth and emerging stage in the development of corporate community relations goes beyond a company's contributions and involvement with charitable organizations. It encompasses how a company operates and what it does in the community—in other words, how it acts as well as its charitable contributions.

The change in expectations and the rise of community stakeholders in determining the company's license to operate constitute the driving force behind this stage. It forces a change in behavior for the company. A company needs to behave in ways that promote and build trust between it and the community. It is not unlike the new relationships between companies and consumers. Consumers' expectations for quality products and services continue to increase. Successful companies develop behaviors that promote the reputation of their products. Many companies use the metaphor "supplier of choice" as a principle to guide this kind of behavior. In turn, they develop courses of action or strategies to become a supplier of choice. Quality programs are examples.

Similarly, the metaphor "employer of choice" is a behavioral principle to guide strategies to attract and retain the brightest and best employees. Wellness programs, work and family accommodations, and even the community reputation of the company are strategies to make a company an employer of choice.

In other words, successful companies have to act in ways that make them a supplier of choice, an employer of choice, and for public companies, an investor of choice. I now add to these principles of success the fourth—neighbor of choice. The term *neighbor of choice* refers to the reputation[28] of the company in the community. Is the company a necessary and desirable asset? Is it sensitive to community concerns? Does it operate its facilities in ways that demonstrate a respect for community concerns? Are the company's actions consistent with its messages? Does it support and contribute to the quality of life in the community? Does the company respect the community's values and traditions? Does it live up to its commitments? Are its actions predictable?

In other words, *can the company be trusted?*

Trust is the critical question and the underlying definition of the neighbor of choice principle. Trust is necessary in developing a positive reputation in the community. Where there is trust, there is respect, a willingness to take someone's expressions and actions at their face value. There are no suspicions, no hidden agendas. Problems and difficulties can be worked out. People who trust each other understand that mistakes can happen, that people will work to correct the mistakes.

Trust cannot be controlled or manipulated. It is based on a company's reputation, which in turn is based on perceptions—how others view the company. Unlike a company's image, therefore, a company's reputation cannot be manipulated, managed, or given a "spin."

Trust is, however, a perishable commodity that needs to be nourished and sustained. It can never be taken for granted. It can never be assumed. It is, as the Canadian Imperial Bank of Commerce advises its managers in its community relations manual for all employees, "earned and comes from being consistent and dependable and doing what we say we will do. Building trust takes time and builds slowly as we begin to show proof of results."[29]

Trust is measurable. Companies that are trusted tend to have respect and good community reputations. They are the admired companies. *Fortune* magazine's annual listing of the top ten companies, for example consistently is composed of companies with excellent community reputations.[30]

The essential aim of becoming a neighbor of choice is to create and build a *legacy* of trust. Stephen Covey calls it a "Personal Integrity Account"—a reserve of trust from which persons can make withdrawals when necessary.[31] There are three ways or strategies for building a legacy of trust or, in other words, for becoming a neighbor of choice:

Build sustainable and ongoing relationships with key community individuals, groups, and organizations

Institute procedures that anticipate and respond to community expectations, concerns, and issues

Focus the community support programs to build relationships, respond to community concerns, and strengthen the community's quality of life (they should also be focused to advance the competitive advantage of the company—described in later chapters)

Build Sustainable Community Relationships

Building sustainable and ongoing relationships in a community is a core strategy for becoming a neighbor of choice. The development of trust depends on respectful relationships. In fact, it is central to the goal of building long-term trust.

Relationships are necessary for a number of reasons. One is to be able to acknowledge and, when necessary, to renegotiate the psychological contract. When Merck, for example, was moving its headquarters to Whitehouse Station in western New Jersey, it sent a community relations representative into the community two years in advance of the move. The community relations manager visited key people in the community along with people who would be living adjacent to the facility. Changes in design were made to comply with the neighbors' requests. As a result, Merck was praised by the mayors of both communities for the way it handled the move. When another company complained that Merck was having little or no difficulty in obtaining its permits, the mayor of Whitehouse Station replied, "Merck does its homework."[32]

Second, companies that have trusting and working relationships in a community are usually given the benefit of the doubt when something unforeseen happens. The residents' response to Merck's accidental chemical release in Albany, Georgia, is one example. Another example is McDonald's Corp. Following the Rodney King acquittal in 1992, parts of Los Angeles were engulfed in a riot. Buildings were burned, looted, and destroyed, including every fast-food restaurant—but McDonald's. None of McDonald's 31 restaurants were burned. When asked why the restaurants were spared, residents and the owner operators talked about the relationships the company had in the community. A video showing the untouched restaurants alongside burned-out buildings is used by the company in its management training programs to demonstrate the importance of community involvement to the company's business.[33]

The media, too, are much more positive toward companies that have good working relationships in a community. In a meeting of business leaders in the Silicon Valley, Rob Elder, vice president and editor of the *San Jose Mercury News*, announced, "We cut some slack with companies that are involved in the community." The paper's policy, he further explained, is to give an opportunity for involved companies to explain their side of a story.[34]

Building relationships is a responsibility of everyone in the company. It cannot be delegated to the public relations staff or community relations managers. It is the managers—CEOs, plant and facility managers, and senior officers—of a company that community representatives want to talk to, not public or community relations officials. The company's managers are the visible representatives of the company. One major criticism leveled at Exxon after the *Valdez* oil spill was that the CEO reportedly was not available and, consequently, did not meet with people in the community. The community became incensed and wanted vengeance. Exxon paid dearly for that mistake.

Relationship building cannot be left to chance. It is a strategy that needs to be implemented by programs and plans.

Identify and Respond to Community Concerns, Issues, and Expectations

A strategy for identifying and responding to community concerns and issues is the second way a company becomes a neighbor of choice. It is the concerns in a community reflected often by key individuals and groups that help a company understand the emerging and important issues in a community.

A company cannot *only* identify and recognize concerns and issues. It also has to acknowledge and respond to them quickly and in a reasonable way. A sincere and genuine response is a way to increase the company's trust account. A company need not acquiesce to every concern. If it has built a trusting relationship, it is able to express its own concerns and negotiate mutually agreeable answers—in other words, be in a position to be able to renegotiate a changing psychological contract.

Many companies have some form of issues management process or procedure to identify and manage emerging issues. Most, however, focus on issues that are societal in scope, affecting potential federal or state legislation. This is a necessary and important area of concern. But frequently community issues are overlooked. An awareness, for example, of the historical concerns of a few influential community residents might have enabled the Disney Company to rethink or even revise its strategy to locate a theme park in northern Virginia.

Another example: Shell U.K. may have been able to divert a public relations and financial disaster if it had conducted an assessment of community concerns in Germany and the United Kingdom at the outset of its planning to decommission the oil rig. Unfortunately, the company did not involve its community relations staff until six months before it started towing the oil rig out into the North Atlantic. And when it did, only three community relations staff were involved. Too little, too late. To its credit, Shell U.K is using the incident to transform itself and be responsive to changing issues and concerns. It has begun a series of surveys identifying needs and opinions in the communities in which it operates. Calling it "reputation management," Shell's strategy consists of "two parallel and interlinked activities: anticipatory issues management and stakeholder relationship building programmes."[35]

Certainly it is not possible or even necessary to replicate an issues management staff in every community. But it is necessary to develop a means for the early identification of issues that have corporate implications. And it is necessary to develop a process and method for assessing community concerns and issues prior to a corporate decision that has implications for a community.

To implement the second strategy of the neighbor of choice, a company needs to develop programs and plans that promote ongoing two-way communication between the company and key individuals and organizations in a community.

Focus on the Community's Concerns and Its Quality of Life

A company takes two kinds of actions that have community implications. A company's primary activities involve the physical movement of raw materials and finished products, the production of goods and services, the marketing and sales of the products, and the after-sales services. (These refer to what Michael Porter calls the company's "value chain," which will be explained in the next chapter.) The way any of these tasks are performed can affect the way the company is viewed in a community and, conceivably, affect its license to operate.

Does the transportation of materials, for example, cause hardships or dangers in the community? Exxon might have avoided the consequences of the *Valdez* oil spill if it had had the foresight to use double-hulled tankers. Are any of its operations—noise, odor, and pollution, for example—offensive to community residents? Do they interfere with the community's quality of life? Does the company offend community sensibilities (note: not an interest group's sensibilities) in the marketing messages? Does the company unfairly target special populations (children, minorities, and disabled, for example) to exploit the sale of its products? Cigarette companies have been justly criticized for using their marketing and sales techniques to influence the smoking habits of young children. This, in turn, has damaged the reputation of the tobacco industry and caused it to lose trust with large segments of the American society. Companies develop what are called community *practice* programs (described in Chapter 8) to respond to the concerns a community has with its operational practices.

Philanthropy or, more properly termed, community *support* programs—donations, voluntarism, product donations, and community partnerships—constitute a company's second type of community actions. These are the most visible, most public, and most expensive elements of a company's involvement in the community. A company's sincerity—fairly or unfairly—is often judged by the nature and extent of its contributions programs. It is the way many companies *and* communities define the responsibility of the company to the community.

As communities redefine their expectations and consequently their relationships with companies, their community support program strategies have to be reshaped and redefined. A company's community support programs need to be able to foster trust relationships in a community, respond to the concerns and needs in a community, and contribute to the community's quality of life. That is the essential strategy for a company's community support programs.

Can a company's community support programs also give it a competitive edge? Can they contribute to the long-term business goals of a company? They certainly can, as I will explain in succeeding chapters.

SUMMARY

The involvement of companies in communities has changed significantly since the 1970s. It has shifted in response to changing community expectations from checkbook philanthropy to a principle about the way a company should behave in a community. Companies now need to act in ways that build community trust—to become neighbors of choice.

To become a neighbor of choice, a company needs to design three strategies and programs of action to implement the principle. They need to:

Build sustainable and ongoing relationships with key community individuals, groups, and organizations

Institute practices and procedures that anticipate and respond to community expectations, concerns, and issues

Focus the community support programs to build relationships, respond to community concerns, and strengthen the community's quality of life

Companies, too, have expectations. They expect to receive value for their involvement. They want the community to provide the services that will enable them to compete in an increasingly competitive and global economy. They want loyalty for their involvement—loyalty of the community, employee, and consumer. They are willing, as the Conference Board found, to use their community programs to create "enhanced public image, increased employee involvement and loyalty, and stronger customer ties."[36]

Fortunately, there have been sufficient shifts in attitudes and behaviors that allow both the company's and the community's expectations to be realized, as I will describe in the next chapter.

NOTES

1. D. B. Henriques, "A Celebrity Boss Faces Exile from 2d Corporate Kingdom," *New York Times*, February 10, 1995, pp. A1, D4; D. B. Henriques, "Ties That Bind: His Directors, Her Charities," *New York Times*, March 21, 1995, p. D1.

2. White House, Executive Order 12329, "President's Task Force on Private Sector Initiatives" (Washington, D.C., 1991).

3. AAFRC Trust, A. E. Kaplan, ed., *Giving USA: The Annual Report on Philanthropy for the Year 1996* (New York: AAFRC Trust for Philanthropy, 1997), pp. 16–21.

4. "Gifts to Nonprofit Groups Rise to a Record But Lag Behind Inflation," *New York Times*, April 27, 1981, pp. B1, B5.

5. C. Marsden, "Community and Educational Relations: Policy Guide Lines," draft, November 1992, p. 2.

6. G. Hiraiwa, "On the Inaugural of Publication of White Paper on Corporate Philanthropy in Japan," in *White Paper on Corporate Philanthropy* (Tokyo: Kiedanren/ Keizai Koho Center, 1992), p. 1.

7. L. V. Gerstner, Jr., R. D. Semerad, D. P. Doyle, and W. B. Johnston, *Reinventing Education: Entrepreneurship in America's Public Schools* (New York: Dutton, 1994), p. 10.

8. "Unions Say AT&T Pact Sets New Standards for Family Benefits," *New York Times*, May 30, 1989, p. A14.

9. See, for example, R. L. Gildea, "Consumer Survey Confirms Corporate Social Action Affects Buying Decisions," *Public Relations Quarterly*, Vol. 39 (Winter 1994–1995), pp. 20–21; Council on Foundations, *Measuring the Value of Corporate Citizenship* (Washington, D.C.: Council on Foundations, 1996).

10. "Denny's and N.A.A.C.P. Reach Agreement on Bias," *New York Times*, May 30, 1993, p. 26; "Denny's Parent Vows Larger Role for Blacks," *New York Times*, July 2, 1993, p. D2.

11. See, for example, S. M. Smith and D. S. Alcorn, "Cause Marketing: A New Direction in the Marketing of Corporate Responsibility," *Journal of Consumer Marketing*, Vol. 8, no. 3 (1991), pp. 19 35; P. N. Bloom, P. Y. Hussein, and L. R. Szykman, "Benefiting Society and the Bottom Line," *Marketing Management*, Vol. 4, no. 3 (Winter 1995), pp. 8–18; K. Dechant and B. Altman, "Environmental Leadership: From Compliance to Competitive Advantage," *Academy of Management Executive*, Vol. 8, no. 3 (1994), pp. 7–19; D. Anfuso, "Creating a Culture of Caring Pays Off," *Personnel Journal*, August 1995, pp. 70–77.

12. C. L. Owen and R. F. Scherer, "Social Responsibility and Market Share," *Review of Business*, Vol. 15, no. 1 (Summer–Fall 1993), pp. 11–16.

13. P. R. Varadaraja and A. Menon, "Cause-Related Marketing: A Coalignment of Marketing Strategy and Corporate Philanthropy," *Journal of Marketing*, Vol. 52 (July 1988), p. 59.

14. Ibid., p. 60.

15. S. M. Smith and D. S. Alcorn, "Cause Marketing: A New Direction in the Marketing of Corporate Responsibility," *Journal of Services Marketing*, Vol. 8, no. 3 (1991), p. 26.

16. Bloom, Hussein, and Szykman, "Benefiting Society and the Bottom Line," pp. 8–18.

17. L. Wagner and R. L. Thompson, "Cause-Related Marketing: Fundraising Tool or Phony Philanthropy," *Nonprofit World*, Vol. 12, no. 6 (November–December 1994), pp. 9–13.

18. P. Goldberg, "Doubts about 'Cause-Related Marketing': A Dangerous Trend in Corporate Giving," *New York Times*, March 29, 1997.

19. "Charities, Corporations Increasing Joint Marketing Activities, However Most Nonprofits Still Out of the Loop," *Responsive Philanthropy*, Winter 1996, p. 11.

20. Research and Forecasts, *The Chivas Regal Report on Working Americans: Emerging Values for the 1990s* (New York: House of Seagram, 1989), p. 107.

21. Ibid., p. 109.

22. Conference Board, *H.R. Executive Review: Competing as an Employer of Choice* (New York: Conference Board, 1996), p. 4.

23. P. Canavan, speech at the Center for Corporate Community Relations at Boston College, Community Relations Leaders Conference, May 9, 1995.

24. W. Safire, "Essay: The New Socialism," *New York Times*, February 26, 1996.

25. D. B. Turban and D. W. Greening, "Corporate Social Performance and Organizational Attractiveness to Prospective Employees," *Academy of Management Journal*, Vol. 40, no. 9 (June 1997), p. 663.

26. J. F. Laabs, "Community Service Helps UPS Develop Managers," *Personnel Journal*, October 1993, pp. 90–98.

27. S. Caudron, "Volunteer Efforts Offer Low-Cost Training Options," *Personnel Journal*, June 1994, pp. 38–43; D. Bollier, "Building Corporate Loyalty While Rebuilding the Community," *Management Review*, October 1996, pp. 17–22.

28. For an excellent book on reputation, see C. J. Fombrun, *Reputation: Realizing the Value from the Corporate Image* (Boston: Harvard Business School Press, 1996).

29. Canadian Imperial Bank of Commerce, *CIBC Community Relations Handbook* (Calgary, Canada: CIBC, 1997).

30. Fombrun, *Reputation*, pp. 187–190.

31. Merck, *A Guide to Becoming a Neighbor of Choice* (White House Station, NJ.: Merck & Co., 1997), p. 9.

32. I. Peterson, "A Company Move That Hasn't Irked the Neighbors," *New York Times*, November 15, 1992, pp. 52, 54.

33. *Wall Street Journal*, November 16, 1992.

34. Rob Elder, vice president and editor, *San Jose Mercury News*, interview with author, March 26, 1998.

35. H. C. Rothermand, letter to the author, June 16, 1997.

36. M. Alperson, quoted in the "Gurin Forum Report," *Giving USA Special Report: Trends in Corporate Philanthropy* (New York: AAFRC Trust for Philanthropy: American Association of Fund-Raising Council, Inc., 1995).

Chapter 3

How to Achieve a Competitive Advantage

In 1955 a handful of engineers left the Sperry Rand Corporation and formed Control Data Corporation. By 1980 they had built the company into a giant in the supercomputer industry. In the space of 25 years Control Data grew in revenues from a little over $600,000 to $4 billion, and from 8 employees to nearly 60,000. It had taken on the giant IBM Corporation and won, including a $101 million lawsuit. Control Data became the world leader in scientific and engineering data services and dominated the independent market for data storage devices. It was a remarkable success, and it was due to the brilliant vision of its founder and CEO, William C. Norris.

At the height of the company's success, Norris proposed another equally challenging vision—to use the talents and resources of the company to solve society's unmet social needs.[1] The idea first came to Norris from a speech he heard by Whitney Young, then national director of the Urban League, on the social and economic injustices against young blacks. Second, and not long after that, race riots erupted in Minneapolis and St. Paul, to the complete surprise of the Twin Cities' business and political leadership. Norris and other business leaders were convinced that they had to become involved in the problems of the Minneapolis and St. Paul inner cities. In other cities where riots had occurred, similar plans were announced.

Under Norris's leadership, Control Data responded by building a plant in the inner city to employ the hard-core unemployed. While it took a few years longer to bring the plant up to the same quality, levels of production, and cost performance of other Control Data facilities, it eventually became successful.

Although the interest of other business leaders in social problems began to wane, Norris continued to follow his vision. He built other plants in inner cities and poor rural areas. He also initiated an ambitious business-education project involving public schools and the University of Illinois to use the computer to improve teaching. This project, called PLATO, began on the basis of Norris's faith in the power of the computer to improve the quality of teaching with digital computers. The company spent over $900 million on the PLATO project in the space of a dozen years. It did not succeed. It failed to convince the education community that computers could be used in teaching. His other social projects began to become costly expenses.

Still believing in the power of the business community to solve social problems, Norris spearheaded the establishment of consortiums of business, religious, and social organizations to work on community problem-solving efforts. He became a national spokesperson on the role of business in addressing society's unmet needs.

Government, which should be responsible for solving social problems, has failed, explained Norris. Social problems continue to grow and, claimed Norris in a speech at MIT on February 19, 1981, "fundamental changes are needed in the way we address society's major needs. One key change," continued Norris, "is for business to take the initiative and provide leadership in planning, managing, and implementing programs designed to meet society's needs and turn them into business opportunities."[2]

Norris's efforts to engage businesses in his campaign met with considerable resistance. He chided his business colleagues for being "inordinately influenced by stockholder pressures to deliver short-term earnings." He lashed out at academia, organized labor, private foundations, and government along with business for their unwillingness to take risks.

In turn, the business community became critical of Norris. An investment banking firm observed that while it was not proper for it "to pass judgment on how appropriate it is for Control Data to spend large amounts of money on social undertakings [the] fact remains that the cost of these projects is preventing operating profits from the business to flow through to the bottom line."[3]

The fortunes of the company began to slip. In 1981 the company's earnings hit a high of $289 million. The next year earnings had dropped to $229 million. Earnings continued to slide until 1985, when it suffered a *loss* of $567 million, just at the time Norris was urging business leaders to join him and assume the responsibility to solve social problems.[4] Norris was forced out as chairman of the company. He was criticized for using the company's assets to pursue social ideas at shareholder expense.[5] According to *Business Week*, Norris frittered "away resources on off beat social schemes and letting grand visions overcome the day-to-day details of running a business for profit."[6]

What happened? Is using the resources of a successful company for community involvement a strategy for disaster? Was Norris ahead of his time?

The answer to both questions is yes.

It is certainly true that the talents within a company can potentially be used to solve community problems. There have been many success stories of corporate involvement in community affairs. The United Way is a case in point.

The modern predecessor to the United Way began in Cleveland by business leaders. Supported by the business community in communities across the United States, it is a fund-raising marvel. Its annual campaigns in which business leaders are heavily involved constitute a major voluntary support of community charities.

The United Way has also been successful in organizing business leaders to work on social issues. Leading chief executive officers such as James Burke of Johnson & Johnson, James Robinson of American Express, and Robert Beck of Prudential Insurance Company, to name a few, were involved in United Way of America Committees persuading the U.S. Congress to pass legislation to feed the poor.

Business involvement in education efforts is showing considerable progress in every major U.S. city. And the business support of employee volunteer efforts has helped to clean up the environment, tutor inner-city schoolchildren, and support a myriad of other social programs and activities. President Jimmy Carter's successful and much admired Habitat for Humanity has the heavy involvement and support of leading businesses.

At the same time, a company has obligations not just to its communities but also to its shareholders, employees, vendors, and customers. Even the staunchest advocates of corporate social responsibility agree that what a company elects to do in a community must not be at the expense of other equally important stakeholders. A company that cannot remain competitive cannot contribute to the community. A company's community strategies and programs, therefore, should be designed to sustain its competitive advantage. Fortunately, the public's shift in attitudes toward corporate community involvement, as described in the last chapter, permits a company to redesign its community programs to contribute to its competitive advantage. It is possible to secure, in the words of David Grayson, of the United Kingdom's Business in the Community, "a win-win" objective—a win for the company and a win for the community. "Corporate community involvement," claims Grayson, "builds people (employees), builds business and it builds a company's license to operate."[7]

Norris's vision, in other words, was ahead of its time. But he also was not guided by the economic imperatives of the company. That is what led to failure. It is now possible to take advantage of the public's new expectations to plan its community programs to meet a community need and to achieve a competitive edge. In this chapter, we want to examine ways this can be done.

COMPETITIVE STRATEGIES

There are, according to Michael Porter, the leading authority on competitive analysis, two core strategies for achieving competitive advantage.[8] One is to be a cost leader, and the second is to produce a product that is highly valued by its buyers. A cost leadership strategy requires a company to keep its costs low in comparison with other producers in its industry. To do this a company needs

Figure 3.1
Porter's Generic Value Chain

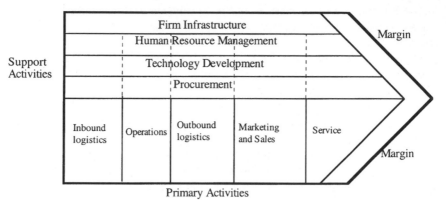

Source: M. Porter, *Competitive Advantage: Creating and Sustaining Superior Performance* (New York: Free Press, 1985), p. 37.

to be *the* low-cost producer. To be the low-cost producer, a company needs to exploit avenues for reducing costs. A company that produces a highly valued product, on the other hand, emphasizes a strategy of differentiation. It wants to position itself as providing a product unique in the industry, so unique that buyers may be willing to pay a premium for its product.

Successful companies emphasize one of the two strategies, but not at the exclusion of the other. A company that follows a differentiation strategy, for example, cannot be heedless of cost factors. At the same time a low-cost producer must pay attention to the quality and reputation of its products.

THE VALUE CHAIN

Porter also claims that competitive advantage cannot be understood without analyzing the tasks a company performs in order to produce a product or service. Labeled the "value chain" it divides a firm into the discrete activities it performs in designing, producing, marketing, and distributing its products. The value chain is the basic tool for diagnosing and enhancing competitive advantage. Each of the activities in the value chain presents opportunities for reducing costs and developing product differentiation strategies. Value is the amount buyers are willing to pay for what a company provides them—a product or service.[9]

Although the value chain of activities for each company is different, every company's value chain is composed of nine different broad categories. Five are termed the *primary activities*, and the other four are *support activities*. See Figure 3.1. The primary activities are those needed to move a product through all its processes from a raw material to a finished product. These can be thought of as the classical managerial functions of a company where there is a manager

Figure 3.2
Definitions of the Activities in Porter's Value Chain

Primary Activities

Inbound logistics: Activities associated with receiving, storing, and disseminating inputs to the product, such as material handling, warehouse inventory control, vehicle scheduling, and return to suppliers.

Operations: Activities associated with transforming inputs into the final product form, such as machining, packaging, assembly, equipment maintenance, testing, printing, and facility operations.

Outbound logistics: Activities associated with collecting and physically distributing the product to buyers, such as finished goods warehousing, material handling, delivery vehicle operation, order processing, and scheduling.

Marketing and sales: Activities associated with providing a means by which buyers can purchase the product and inducing them to do so, such as advertising, promotion, sales force, quoting, channel selection, channel relations, and pricing.

Service: Activities associated with providing service to enhance or maintain the value of the product, such as installation, repair, training, parts supply, and product adjustment.

Support Activities

Procurement: The function of purchasing inputs, such as purchasing of raw materials, supplies, and other consumable items as well as assets such as machinery, equipment, and buildings.

Technology development: Know-how, procedures, and technical inputs needed to improve the products and the process.

Human resource management: Activities involved in the recruiting, hiring, training, development, and compensation of all types of personnel.

Firm infrastructure: Consists of a number of activities including general management, planning, finance, accounting, legal, government affairs, and quality management.

Source: M. Porter, *Competitive Advantage: Creating and Sustaining Superior Performance* (New York: Free Press, 1985), pp. 39–43.

in charge of each of the tasks.[10] These activities (listed along the bottom of the figure) include the physical creation of the product and its sale and transfer to the buyer as well as after-sale assistance.

Support activities support the primary activities and each other by providing purchased inputs, technology, human resources, and company-wide functions. The dotted line indicates that procurement, technology development, and human resource management can be associated with specific primary activities as well as the entire range of activities. The company's infrastructure supports all the activities of the value chain. Figure 3.2 provides definitions of the primary and support activities.[11] The activities in the value chain are the building blocks, discrete building blocks, claims Porter, that a company uses to create a product valuable to its buyers and, thus, achieve a competitive advantage. They determine whether a company is a high- or low-cost producer and the value of the product to the buyer or how the product is differentiated in the marketplace.

CONTROLLING COST DRIVERS

There are a number of ways that a company's community practices, or the way in which it designs its community programs, can be used to reduce costs. The most obvious activities are those related to maintaining the company's license to operate in local communities. These are part of the company's infrastructure activities in the value chain. Porter, for example, comments that for telephone operating companies "negotiating and maintaining relations with regulatory bodies can be among the most important activities for [their] competitive advantage."[12]

These kinds of relationships now have to be broadened beyond government regulatory agencies. All companies have to engage in relationship building activities with a variety of individuals and groups in a community. It is not, as Porter suggests, an important activity, but it is now an essential activity for creating trust and consequently maintaining the license to operate. A company cannot compete sucessfully if its freedom to operate is hindered.

Equally essential are the environmental and nuisance impacts of the company's operations in a community. These are activities that can affect the costs of operation. Porter calls these "institutional cost" drivers that can lead to expensive laws and regulations. Very often laws and regulations are the result of changing attitudes toward a company's operation—nuisance factors, for example, such as noise, odors, and traffic patterns that cause inconvenience to community residents.

Environmental attitudes and the resulting regulations at both federal and local levels are classic examples of the impact of an institutional cost driver on companies. Environmental costs to companies rose so dramatically and so quickly in the 1980s and 1990s that companies and trade associations, such as the Chemical Manufacturers Association, set up committees and task forces to deal with the growing regulatory forces.

Initially companies responded by trying to control and influence the increasing environmental regulations. The growing pressures from society and the demands from all sources in society to control environmental pollution, however, required companies to go beyond "fire fighting and a reliance on band aid solutions," according to one study.[13] The publicity and subsequent heavy fines imposed on Exxon, GE, CSX, and Union Carbide became a wake-up call for many companies to control environmental costs. Pitney Bowes, for example, discovered that between 1984 and 1989 the per drum costs of hazardous waste disposal escalated five times to a total cost of $16.3 million.[14]

The best practice is to integrate environmental compliance with organizational strategy. Firms such as Johnson & Johnson, Procter & Gamble, Lever Brothers, Pitney Bowes, IBM, Olin, and Colgate-Palmolive have integrated environmentalism into their business planning and operations in ways that translate into bottom-line benefits. This represents a newer thinking from compliance to making environmental thinking a part of corporate strategy and moving from defensive tactics to viewing improving environmental performance as a competitive advantage.[15]

To remain competitive a company has to respond to the institutional cost drivers. To gain a competitive advantage, a company can go beyond the environmental requirements and proactively operate the firm as an environmental leader. This is an optional strategy that is aimed at creating trust in a community. It is also an optional strategy to differentiate a company and its products in the marketplace.

There are other community program practices that a company can include in its value chain activities to control costs and improve its competitive advantage. After discovering, for example, that low-income customers represented 5 percent of the service population but 40 percent of its uncollectible debts, Baltimore Gas and Electric partnered with a counseling service of the state human services department and set up the Baltimore Crisis Center to give advice on budget planning. The networking model not only helped reduce unpaid utility bills, according to the company, but also enhanced customer confidence and self-respect. Its success led to the establishment of another crisis center and earned the company a Special Distinction Award from the Edison Electric Institute.

SAFECO, the second largest property and casualty insurer in the United States, provides another example and one that integrates cost-saving preventive programs with building trust relationships with community organizations. SAFECO is well aware, not unlike many other insurers, that preventive programs can have a marked affect on reducing claims. Prevention has become a major cost-reducing strategy employed by all sorts of insurance companies. Companies that insure workers' compensation claims, for example, spend considerable sums on worker safety programs. SAFECO, an industry leader in fire, crime, and safety prevention, has for years used the traditional public relations and awareness programs to educate its clients. It also gave donations to community organizations and agencies including volunteer firefighters. This is a fairly common approach in the home insurance industry.

In the early 1990s the company began to look again at the urban market, particularly at urban neighborhoods for growth and profit potential. An article by Michael Porter in the *Harvard Business Review* gave support for the development of an urban market strategy. According to Porter, the inner city was a poorly served market with significant potential, particularly for retailing, financial services, and personal services. "Boston's inner city, for example," claimed Porter, "has an estimated total family income of $3.4 billion. . . . In addition the market is young and growing rapidly, owing in part to immigration and relatively high birth rates."[16]

To become involved in urban neighborhoods meant finding ways to establish relationships. SAFECO came up with an innovative idea that it called the Neighborhood Safety Impact Program. Community-based organizations were given grants for developing programs focusing on appearance, crime prevention, home safety, and maintenance. This in turn would assist in improving the insurability of these homes and businesses. The innovative part of the program is that SA-FECO involved their underwriting, marketing, and claims staff in the design of the projects and identifying organizations to receive grants. SAFECO insists that the real value of the program is to ''create opportunities to get to know neighborhoods and residents on a personal level, changing perceptions and fostering new ideas and attitudes.''[17] This enables the company to use relationship selling and to be the low-cost producer in expanding new markets in urban neighborhoods across the country.

Another cost-reducing strategy is to use community support programs to reduce human resource management costs. This has become an increasingly popular strategy in companies. Thom McAn and UPS, as I pointed out earlier, have developed volunteer programs to provide experiential learning on diversity issues for their managers. UPS has established a ''Community Internship Program'' to manage these initiatives.

These types of programs have led companies to involve community relations personnel in the performance development of managers. Working together, the community relations and human resource staff match managers with volunteer activities that can lead to improving management skills. This has become a popular practice in the United Kingdom. Companies loan managers to community organizations for skill development. Some are loaned on a three- to six-month basis full-time. Others are loaned one day a week for three months.

Another and increasingly popular technique is to engage groups of workers in one-day or weekend volunteer projects to promote teamwork. An interesting example is a program that was used by GE Plastics to promote team building and integration among two different companies. In 1988, GE Plastics, headquartered in Pittsfield, Massachusetts, purchased one of its longtime competitors, Borg-Warner Chemicals, in West Virginia. Naturally, there were morale problems as well as heightened suspicions in bringing together two dissimilar cultures and management personalities. Traditionally, GE depended upon business meetings in warm climate cities involving golf tournaments and sporting events to build employee morale and loyalty. This was the planned format for the company's 1989 annual meeting to be held in San Diego. One main agenda item was to build trust and loyalty with the Borg-Warner employees.

Because of the differences in culture between the two companies, the usual format was shelved. The company decided to engage the employees of both companies—over 450—in a fix-up and repair of a YMCA in a low-income neighborhood of San Diego. In twelve hours, 99 percent of the renovation was completed. It was, according to one manager, the turning point in the integration of GE Plastics and Borg-Warner. Its success has spread to other companies within GE. At a GE retreat in Miami, for example, Robert Wright, CEO of

NBC, recruited 160 executives to work with him in refurbishing a day care center in the Coconut Grove neighborhood.[18]

A still further technique to reduce costs is to integrate community relations and community programming with business policy development and implementation. Merck, as we noted in Chapter 2, for example, reduced its permitting time in half (from 18 months to 9 months) when it put a community relations manager in a community two years in advance of moving a facility. This resulted in considerable savings in legal fees and management time to attend permitting hearings.

Some companies form committees or panels of community residents to advise the company on policy decisions. The goal of these programs is to develop trust relationships. But they also are an early warning program and serve the purpose of avoiding costs that can arise from making decisions that can bring about community opposition.

PRODUCT DIFFERENTIATION

Differentiating a company's product in the marketplace is, according to strategy theorists Hax and Majluf, "a most critical factor in the determination of competitive rivalry. Nothing could be more devastating to industry profitability than the 'commodity syndrome.' A commodity is a product or service that cannot be differentiated. That means that no one can legitimately claim that what it is offering to its customers is superior to an equivalent offering from other companies."[19] This is why companies are so eager to differentiate their products by brand names. "Brand identity," say Hax and Majluf, "constitutes an important source of differentiation and, therefore, firms try to establish solidly their brands in the market. Brand recognition by consumers is eagerly sought by most companies, and they spend dearly for it."[20]

Corporate reputation, which is the perception of the company to those on the outside, is widely accepted as a means of improving brand image. Traditionally, reputation was judged only on measurable factors such as financial performance and product quality. Now surveys conducted by the The Economist and Fortune magazine include community and environmental responsibility as criteria for a corporate reputation. Dragon International, a London-based brand development and corporate reputation research organization, advises its clients based on its own research, "There is an opportunity for companies to achieve competitive advantage through corporate reputation." Dragon goes on to say, "Companies can achieve competitive advantage by being seen by consumers to be innovative in areas such as environment, employee welfare, fair trading, *community involvement*, and ethical marketing"[21] (my emphasis). They advise their clients to tie corporate reputation with brand identification.

Grey Advertising offers similar advice to its worldwide clients. "Consumers are intensely concerned with the source of the brands they buy—they're taking their desire for quality-of-life control to the marketplace." They are using "responsible community citizenship'' as a guide for brand loyalty, Grey goes on to add.[22]

What Dragon, Grey, and other advertising firms are saying is that consumers are influenced by what Porter calls *signaling criteria*. Signaling criteria reflect the signals of value that influence the buyer's perception of the product or service. Signaling criteria can include not only such traditional activities as advertising, packaging, appearance of product, and time in business but also the activities of the firm. These activities can include the performance of the company in the community. Performance signaling criteria could include the value the company attaches to operating in an environmentally responsible manner. It can include, also, the direct involvement of the company in the quality-of-life issues and needs of communities and societies.

Signaling criteria are most important when buyers have a difficult time assessing a product's performance. They have no way of determining if the product or service will perform as the company purports it will. Many electronic products, for example, are only marginally different in price, and all look and appear to perform alike. There is no way of judging their value. Other products and services are also difficult to differentiate on the basis of the quality of the product.

Consequently, the reputation of the company in the community has become an added and important signaling criterion. And if it is an important criterion for competitive advantage, it needs to be made known to the buyer. It needs to be communicated. The Porter framework is a useful guide to identifying activities of a community relations nature that can be included in the company's value chain. Figure 3.3 is an illustration of some of the activities a company can use to achieve a competitive advantage.

It is no accident, therefore, that companies are advertising or ''signaling'' their involvement in the community as a differentiating strategy to achieve a competitive advantage in the marketplace. Raytheon, Prudential Insurance Company, and IBM, for example, publicize the work of employee volunteers in full-page newspaper ads. Brooks Brothers advertises a scholarship award program in leading newspapers. Benneton organizes a consumer drive for used clothing for the needy. Mobil runs recurring ads in the op-ed page of the *New York Times* and frequently describes its philanthropy efforts. Colgate uses inserts in newspapers to tell customers about the Starlight Foundation, which fulfills fantasies for sick and dying children. According to Colgate, it is ''a terrific promotion that both sells and shows that Colgate cares.'' Travelodge uses its community relations as a foundation for its marketing and business strategies.[23]

Cause-related marketing is another example and a very direct use of signaling criteria to differentiate a brand in the marketplace. The attractiveness of cause marketing is that it not only builds brand recognition, but it also contributes to increasing the community reputation of the company.

Figure 3.3
Examples of Neighbor of Choice Programs That Can Contribute to a Company's Value Chain

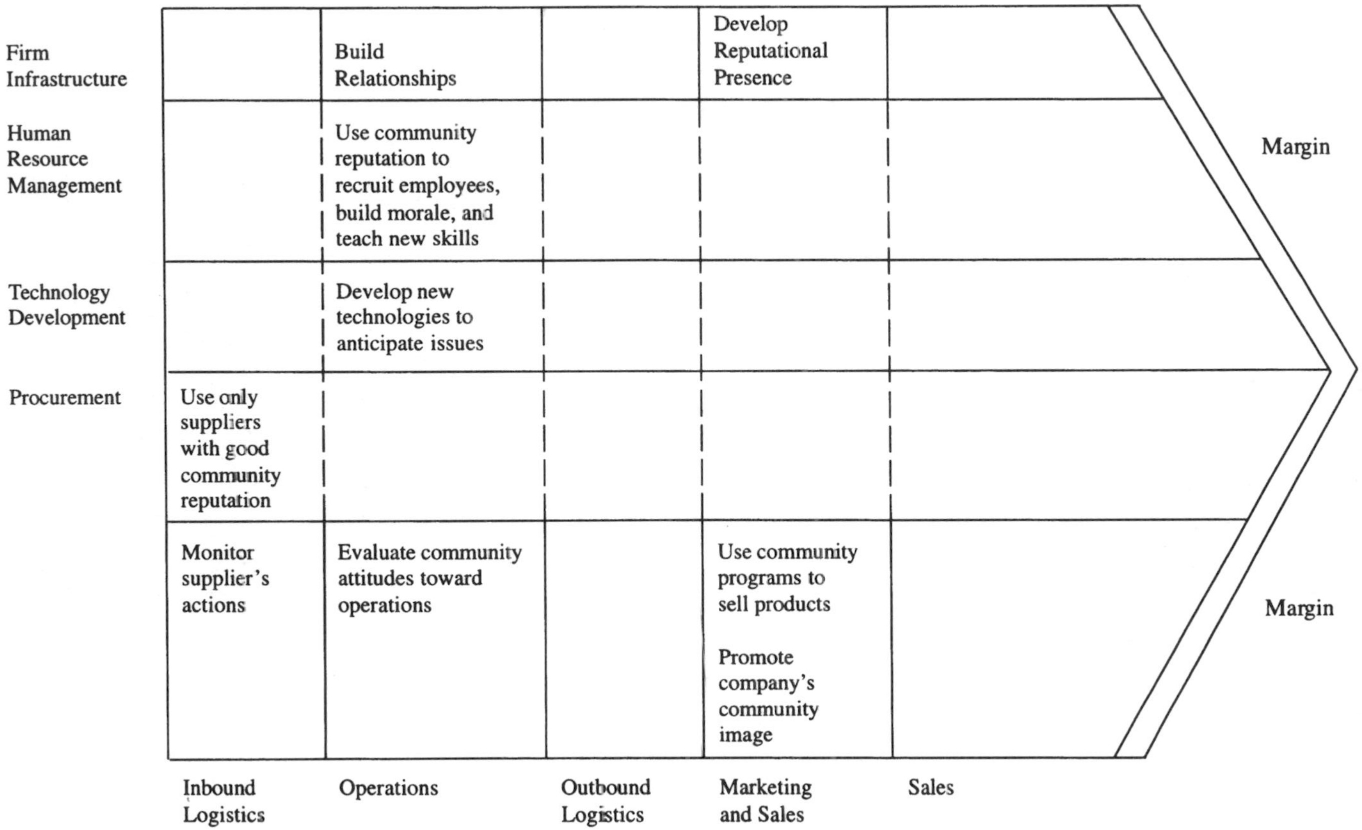

	Inbound Logistics	Operations	Outbound Logistics	Marketing and Sales	Sales
Firm Infrastructure		Build Relationships		Develop Reputational Presence	
Human Resource Management		Use community reputation to recruit employees, build morale, and teach new skills			
Technology Development		Develop new technologies to anticipate issues			
Procurement	Use only suppliers with good community reputation				
	Monitor supplier's actions	Evaluate community attitudes toward operations		Use community programs to sell products Promote company's community image	

Margin

Margin

Figure 3.4
Driving Forces for Neighbor of Choice

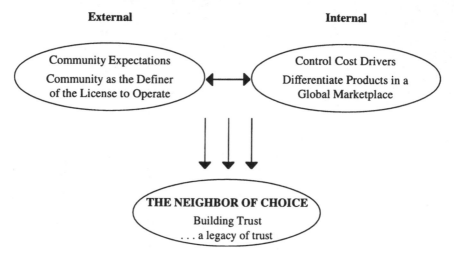

SUMMARY

While the changes in attitudes and expectations toward corporate behavior have influenced a company's license to operate, they have also presented companies with strategic opportunities. They provide ways for companies to reduce costs and to differentiate their products and services in the marketplace. They are, in other words, business opportunities, graphically depicted in Figure 3.4.

NOTES

1. J. C. Worthy, "Introduction," in W. C. Norris, *New Frontiers for Business Leadership* (Minneapolis: Dorn Books, 1983), pp. 17–41. See also J. C. Worthy, *William C. Norris: Portrait of a Maverick* (Cambridge, MA: Ballinger Publishing Co., 1987).

2. Norris, *New Frontiers for Business Leadership*, p. 49.

3. Worthy, *William C. Norris*, p. 4.

4. Ibid., pp. 12–13.

5. Ibid., p. 203.

6. P. Houston and G. Boch, "Can Gentleman Farmer Get Control Data Out of the Ditch?" *Business Week*, January 27, 1986, p. 45.

7. D. Grayson, "Corporate Citizenship: What They Should Teach You at the Harvard Business School (And Other Schools, Too!)," unpublished report of a symposium between business and business schools at Durdent Court, Denham, England, November 1995.

8. M. Porter, *Competitive Advantage: Creating and Sustaining Superior Performance* (New York: Free Press, 1985), pp. 11–16.

9. Ibid., p. 26.

10. A. C. Hax and N. S. Majluf, *The Strategy Concept and Process: A Pragmatic Approach* (Englewood Cliffs, NJ: Prentice-Hall, 1991), p. 78.

11. M. Porter, *Competitive Advantage*, pp. 39–43.

12. Ibid, p. 43.

13. K. Dechant and B. Altman, "Environmental Leadership: From Compliance to Competitive Advantage," *Academy of Management Executive*, Vol. 8, no. 3 (1994), p. 8.

14. Ibid.

15. Ibid., pp. 7–19.

16. M., Porter, "The Competitive Advantage of the Inner City," *Harvard Business Review*, May–June 1995, pp. 55–71.

17. G. C. Hamilton, vice president, SAFECO Insurance Company of America, speech at Corporate Involvement in Community and Economic Development Seminar, The Center for Corporate Community Relations at Boston College, September 11, 1997.

18. D. Bollier, "Building Corporate Loyalty While Rebuilding the Community," *Management Review*, October 1996, pp. 17–22.

19. Hax and Majluf, *The Strategy Concept and Process*, p. 39.

20. Ibid., p. 40.

21. Dragon International, *Corporate Reputation: Does the Consumer Care?* (London: Dragon International, n.d.), pp. 1, 3.

22. Grey Advertising, Inc., *Grey Matter Alert No. 3: Today's Americans, in Tough Times and Beyond* (New York: Grey Advertising, 1991), p. 4.

23. Phillips Business Information, Inc., "Personifying Corporate America with Community Programs," *PR News*, Vol. 54, no. 2 (January 19, 1988).

Part II

Implementing
the Neighbor of Choice

Chapter 4

The Company Assessment

The term *neighbor of choice* is a metaphor, as I explained in Chapter 2, that describes how a company should be positioned in a community. Some companies find the term helpful in defining how they want to be perceived in the community. Some use the term or a variation of it in describing their community relations strategies and programs (see Figure 4.1). Others do not. Nonetheless, most companies, as a consequence of the changes described in the first part of this book, are redesigning and reengineering all or a major part of their community relations activities and programs. The neighbor of choice principle is a guide—albeit a necessary and useful guide.

INTERNAL AND EXTERNAL ASSESSMENTS

There are three program strategies for implementing the neighbor of choice: relationship building, identifying concerns and issues, and designing community programs. In order for a company to design these strategies, it needs to conduct both an internal and an external assessment. Both of these assessments should be able to describe how the company is, and wants to be, positioned in the community.

How extensive the assessment should be will depend on the amount of information the company has on the way it is currently positioned in the community and the resources it wants to spend on the assessment. What is described here is a comprehensive list of elements to be used as a guide in conducting the company and community assessments.

THE COMPANY ASSESSMENT

Designing neighbor of choice strategies begins with a company or organizational assessment. The purpose of the assessment is to answer four questions:

Figure 4.1
Sample of Companies Using the Term "Neighbor of Choice" to Describe Community Relations

AMP	Merck & Co., Inc.	Phillips Petroleum
British Airways	Motorola	Rockwell International
Diageo	Northern Illinois Gas	Shell Chemical
EDS	Olin Chemical	Sprint
Genzyme, Inc.	Pacific Gas & Electric	State Street Bank

Where are we now?

Where do we want to be?

What community attitudes can interfere with any of our value chain activities?

How do we create commitment to carrying out the company's community relations planning goals?

The first three are planning questions. What information does the company have about its current community relationships activities and community programs? Second, how does the company want to be viewed in the community? The fourth question relates to coordination, or making certain that the planning decisions, once accepted, are adopted by all members of the organization. Coordination need not wait, however, until a plan is developed. It can and should be part of the planning process. It is an axiom of effective planning that those that "do" should do the planning. To be committed to planning goals demands that managers be engaged in a journey that shapes the course and results of planning. When they are engaged, claims Henry Mintzberg, a leading writer and researcher on business and strategic planning, the enthusiasm and commitment build along the way.[1]

Neighbor of choice is a *corporate-wide* principle, not a community relations principle. Consequently, it has to be implemented by managers, not specialists or planners. The manager's commitment and involvement in the development of the strategies and plans for implementing the neighbor of choice principle are essential. Otherwise it will not happen. The internal assessment, therefore, needs to be both a procedure—steps that have to be taken in the development of strategies and plans—and a process, or what Mintzberg refers to as a style of planning. The process should be designed in a way that encourages the involvement of the managers accountable for creating trust between the community and the company.

Many companies have established advisory committees of managers from various functions to participate in the design and operation of the community relations program and the company assessment. Some community relations managers deliberately include managers who are skeptical about the value of com-

Figure 4.2
The Elements of the Factual Information for a Company Assessment

---

Factual

Contributions

Volunteerism

Partnerships

Policies

---

munity relations. "It is one of the best techniques I know of," according to Ann Pomykal, State and Community Affairs manager for Texas Instruments, Inc., "for creating acceptance for community relations' goals and objectives."[2]

Three categories of information need to be collected in conducting an internal or organizational assessment. One is factual information—actual data on specific company programs or practices. How much money is the company donating to the community? and How many volunteers are active in the community on behalf of the company? are two examples of factual data.

Second, the company needs information about the attitudes and impressions of what the company is doing in the community. This is qualitative information—judgments from key managers and employees on their perceptions of the company's image, for example.

A third category is information that is strategic in nature. Specifically, the objective is to identify the strengths and weaknesses of the company's community relations efforts.

Obtaining Factual Information

Factual information is obtained by conducting audits of the company's charitable contributions, employee volunteer programs, and its partnerships with community-based organizations (Figure 4.2). An analysis of the policies and procedures related to community relations is also part of the factual assessment.

Conducting a contributions audit reveals surprising results. Few companies actually know how much money and products they are contributing to charitable causes unless they conduct a company-wide audit. Over 50 percent of companies reporting on their contributions to the Conference Board cannot give an exact figure on the amount of the company's contributions to charities.

Contributions audits, conducted across the company, often reveal a significant number of unreported donations. It is not uncommon, for example, for the purchasing department to make donations to charitable causes on behalf of major vendors, for the marketing department to buy tickets for charitable dinners hosted by important buyers, or for plant managers to donate to a number of local causes in addition to the major charities supported by the company.

How much is unreported? It is difficult to say, because very few companies collect all of this information. It can range, however, from a few thousand dollars to millions. The former president of a major bank in Boston, for example, learned that the company was contributing money outside of its foundation only after a vendor at a company function thanked the CEO for the company's generous $20,000 donation to a favorite charity.

The manager of the American Honda Foundation, Kathy Carey, decided in 1995 to conduct a full audit of all department donations and found that they were underreporting donations in the millions of dollars. The CEO believed that the company's donations amounted to $4 million to $5 million over a three-year period. The foundation manager discovered that it was in excess of $100 million. The company has since improved its auditing procedures and proudly publicizes to the community that it makes annual contributions of between $33 million and $34 million.[3]

An audit of contributions is also valuable for accountability purposes. After Ashley DesMartens, manager of Educational Programs of Intel Corporation's Folsom, California site, conducted a routine audit of its contributions, it was discovered that a gift of computers and a donation of $25,000 were going to the personal use of a principal and teacher. Intel and the city's school administration quickly put into place policies and procedures to avoid the fraudulent use of corporate contributions.[4]

Gifts of products or "in-kind" donations is another type of charitable contribution commonly made by companies. And while it can be quantified, the base on which it is quantified varies from one company to another. Some companies, for example, report product donations on the basis of its cost to produce the product, others on the wholesale cost, others on the general retail cost, and still others on the "suggested" retail price. The absence of any agreed-upon standard has generated controversy. The *Wall Street Journal* reported that major computer companies, such as IBM, Lotus, Microsoft, and Novell, are fighting among each other over the value assigned to gifts of software after the Taft Giving Directory calculated that Microsoft had replaced IBM as the top corporate giver in the United States in 1996.[5]

There is also no agreement on how to define in-kind donations. Some companies count their loaned executive costs as a product donation. Others consider loaned executives as volunteers.

The absence of an agreed-upon standard for charitable contributions is a weakness in corporate community relations. Companies, for example, are unable to compare their contributions with other companies. They are forced to make planning decisions without some very important information. It is comparable to making pricing decisions without knowing what other companies are charging for the same product or service. A solution to this problem, which is outside the scope of this book, is needed for effective community relations planning.

A second kind of quantifiable information is a company's volunteer activities. The objective is to get data on the extent and scope of employee volunteer activities. How many employees are volunteering and in what activities and organizations? It is useful to determine, too, the barriers to volunteering. Knowing what prevents employees from volunteering is necessary in planning volunteer programs.

Companies report that measuring the extent and scope of employee volunteering is difficult. Some employees are reluctant to respond to surveys or questions about their volunteer activities. They believe that volunteerism is a personal responsibility and not any business of the company. Obviously, these opinions need to be respected. It is possible, however, to increase reporting on surveys of volunteer activities over time once employees learn that the purpose of the surveys is to improve employee volunteer programs. One way this is communicated is through reports of survey results in a timely fashion. If there is any iron law of survey research, it is this: Always report back survey results—and report them back as quickly as possible.

A third kind of quantifiable information is the scope of partnership programs with community-based organizations. Business-community partnerships, particularly business-education partnerships, are popular methods for improving the effectiveness of a company's contributions efforts. Many companies report, however, that they are not satisfied with their partnership programs. The goals of the partnerships from the company's perspective are not realized. "A lot of effort, for too little results," is the common complaint.

A fourth kind of quantitative information is a description of the policies and procedures that guide the company's external affairs programs. All companies have policies governing their contributions programs to meet legal requirements. Most also publish guidelines that describe the company's contributions programs.

A growing number of companies have policies that guide their volunteer programs. These are policies that describe the amount of time an employee can take off to engage in company-sponsored volunteer activities. The Lotus Corporation, for example, allows a day off a month for volunteer activities. AT&T is another company that allows paid time off for all its employees for volunteer work. Other companies allow time off but leave it up to the discretion of the supervisor as to when and how often it is allowed.

Assessing the programs and practices of the company should be done annually. It should form the basis of a report on what the company is doing in the community as well as a part of the company's community relations program planning. The factual assessment should be compiled by the community relations staff.

Qualitative Information

Information on how the company perceives it is positioned in the community is important for uncovering myths, explicit and implicit expectations of the community, and attitudes that can interfere with program planning. These are judgments, and that is the reason they are categorized as qualitative information. The primary stakeholders who should be involved in supplying qualitative information are the CEO, senior officers, operating managers, community relations managers, and employees.

CEO. Over the past 30 years there has been an astounding shift in the role and responsibilities of CEOs. At one time the function was 60 to 70 percent internal, the ''getting things done,'' in the organization. This has been reversed. CEOs are viewed as the principal spokespeople of the company and the personification of its reputation. The community, the public, and the press look to the CEO for explanations of corporate practices and behavior, regardless of who is at fault. Often, too, this has ramifications for the CEO's family.

When, for example, the CEO of a Boston bank was subpoenaed to appear before a congressional committee to explain alleged violations in lending practices, his immediate neighbors cautioned their children not to discuss this problem with the banker's children. Of course, the neighbor's children did not heed their parents' advice and curiously discussed it with the banker's children. The CEO then had to explain the issue and problem to his own children.

For many reasons, therefore, the CEO, along with the board, has to be involved in the formation of the values and framework underlying the external affairs philosophy and strategies. The kinds of information that need to be sought from a CEO are related to the external affairs vision and strategy. How does the CEO and the company's board want the company to be viewed in the community? What does the CEO and the board want people in the community to say about the company? Equally important, what don't they want the community to say about the company?

There are also questions of positioning. What does the CEO look for from the community? What attitudes, programs, and services are needed from the community to maintain or advance the competitive advantage of the company? What does the CEO believe are the expectations of the community—implicitly as well as explicitly? How should the company position itself in the community? What should be the major community programs that help to promote the quality of life in the community for its residents as well as the company's employees? In other words, what contribution in money, human resources, and spirit should the company make to the community?

The CEO should also provide information about the relationship of the company's values to its community programs. How can the company demonstrate its own core values and uniqueness through its community programs?

An assessment of the CEO's willingness and readiness to commit the company to implementing the neighbor of choice strategies has to be obtained. What kind of commitment in resources and time is the CEO and the company's senior officers willing to make in order to implement a corporate-wide set of strategies to implement the neighbor of choice principle?

For some companies, the commitment is forced on them by external events. Shell, for example, viewed the Brent Spar incident as, the managing director called it, "an icon" mandating change.[6] This is what prompted the worldwide assessment of the company's community reputation, referred to earlier. Other companies are adopting the neighbor of choice principle in response to their assessment of the changing demands of communities, at the advice and suggestion of colleagues, or as a consequence of internal pressures from operating managers and community relations managers.

On the other hand, some CEOs or senior managers are not ready or willing to commit the company to a corporate-wide strategy change. They prefer to move cautiously and incrementally. There is nothing wrong with using incrementalism in the development of corporate-wide strategies. In fact, one scholar of business planning, James Brian Quinn, believes on the basis of his research that strategy evolves in an incremental fashion, not as a consequence of a grand design.[7]

Regardless of whether the development of the neighbor of choice strategies is a process of incrementalism or part of a major strategic overhaul as a consequence of an incident of community opposition, the CEO and senior officers' commitment needs to be assessed before embarking on the road to planning.

Senior officers. Senior officers are a second set of internal stakeholders who need to be involved in supplying information and direction to the company's external affairs strategies. Senior officers have to hold accountable the managers responsible for implementing community relations programs and actions. They need to communicate to managers that community relations encompass not only charitable donations but the way a company has to do business in a changing society.

The kinds of information that need to be obtained from senior officers are:

Willingness and readiness to commit to a shift in strategy to the neighbor of choice

Current involvement in community programs and activities, particularly involvement in leadership positions

Attitudes toward the community

Expectations of what the community should provide to the company

Assessment and quality of their relationships with key people in the community (it is sometimes helpful to scale responses from 1, very good, to 5, very poor, for this information)

Opinion on the programs in the community that are necessary for meeting quality-of-life needs of their employees and families

The kind of activities and programs that will contribute to advancing the competitive advantage of the company

Suggestions on the kinds of community organizations and programs that should be supported by the company

Site and facility managers. These operating managers are a third informational source needed for information in the planning and design of a company's external affairs strategies. Facility managers are the front-line representatives of the company. People in communities do not make relationships with companies or organizations but with people in companies and organizations. Knowledge of the extent and quality of facility managers' relationships in the community is critical to the development of relationship building programs. The facility manager is also one of the best sources of information on community concerns and issues and the attitudes of people in the community toward the company.

The facility managers or their representatives in the company are often the individuals who have to respond to the concerns of the community. When there are concerns about a company's operating practices or about its future policies, the press and community representatives look to the facility manager for answers. The facility manager needs to have the skills to respond effectively to these concerns.

The facility manager is also a source of information about community expectations. The facility manager's relationships and involvement in community activities are a rich source of information about changing expectations.

Community relations managers. The function of community relations managers has changed profoundly in the past 20 years. Although a community relations manager was once primarily a representative of the company at community events and an adviser to the CEO on contributions decisions, his or her role has evolved to include a variety of management responsibilities. In most companies today, community relations managers are viewed as the technical experts on communities—community needs, emerging issues, the key community leaders—and on how community decisions are made. Because of their collaboration and involvement with colleagues from other companies and their participation in professional associations, they have knowledge, too, about current and emerging trends and practices in community relations of companies around the world.

The kind of information that community relations managers can provide in conducting an internal assessment are:

Attitudes and expectations of community representatives toward the company in comparison to other companies in the community

Community relations trends and practices

Emerging community and societal trends likely to affect the functions and practices of community relations

Assessment of community needs obtained from primary and secondary sources

Adequacy of community programs and services

Employees. Employees are the bulk users of community services and programs. Consequently, employee evaluations of needs and services in a community constitute valuable information for planning. They are also excellent sources of information on community attitudes toward the company. Companies

Figure 4.3
The Elements of the Factual and the Qualitative Information for a Company Assessment

Factual	Qualitative
Contributions	Willingness to plan
Volunteerism	Relationships in community
Partnerships	Community needs, attitudes,
Policies	and expectations

such as Boeing regularly conduct surveys of employees to obtain information on community needs and attitudes. Other companies depend upon focus groups or advisory committees composed of employees and managers to gather information on needs and attitudes as well as guidance on the company's community contributions programs.

But surveying employees for information on the community is equally, if not more, important as a means for promoting employee loyalty. Studies of employee attitudes toward a company's reputation in the community reveal that the involvement of the company in community affairs is highly valued. Over two thirds of employees consider community involvement an important indicator of their loyalty, as I described in Chapter 2. The same studies also reveal that of less than 50 percent of employees know anything about the contributions or the involvement of the company in the community.[8]

One of the best ways to communicate to employees about the company's concern and interests toward the community is to survey them for their opinions on what the company should do. It is without a doubt the most inexpensive way to demonstrate to the employees that the company cares about the community and that it needs their opinions on what programs should be developed to respond to community needs.

The function of the qualitative assessment is to gather information on five basic elements. One is the willingness and readiness of the company to engage in designing neighbor of choice strategies. The second is a listing of the existing relationships between the selected managers and community groups and organizations. If possible, it is helpful to assess the quality of the relationships, even if it is only personal judgments. The third is an assessment of the needs and services in the community as determined by the employees and selected managers. A fourth is the perception of the attitudes of the community toward the company. And the fifth is the perception of the community's expectations of the company and the company's expectations of the community (see Figure 4.3).

The development of the qualitative assessment is a company-wide effort and should be the responsibility of a senior officer. Parts of the assessment can be compiled on an ongoing basis, but it is an assessment that should be conducted every three to five years.

Strategic Information: Defining Strengths and Weaknesses

The third category of information conducted in the internal assessment is strategic in intent. The focus is on identifying the strengths and weaknesses of the company in the community and its community relations activities and programs. This is the place, too, for identifying community practices that are likely to hinder its license to operate. Also, strategic information should be used to point out opportunities for using community programs for competitive advantage.

Companies can bring different strengths to their community programming. Technology companies, for example, have unique strengths in the technical skills of their employees that can be used to improve community programs. The annual ''Net Day'' in which technology companies have joined together to provide the wiring to the Internet for public schools is a good example.

Assessing the strengths of the community relations programs is also necessary in compiling information for planning neighbor of choice strategies. In some companies, the strength lies in the involvement of senior managers in the community. The CEO's access to community officials through involvement in community problem-solving activities is an effective way to promote relationships of trust.

Assessing the company's weaknesses in the community is equally important in the design of neighbor of choice strategies. What is the nature and strength of the company's relationships with key organizations and officials? Is the company viewed as an asset? Does it have trust?

Owing to the increased importance of community services to a company's business goals and aims, the relationship of services to goals requires examination. What community services need to be established or improved to meet the company's business aims? Does, for example, the education system need to be improved? Do services or programs exist in the community that can be used to improve the competitive advantage of the company? How can programs be developed to make use of these services?

A company also has to be realistic in identifying the weaknesses of the community relations programs. Is it adequately funded in comparison to other companies in the industry? Is the staff capable of carrying out the new demands of a corporate-wide strategy?

As companies move their community relations strategy from a focus on community programs to a corporate-wide strategy of promoting the company as a neighbor of choice, the functions of community relations will shift significantly. Companies have relied on the community relations staff to position the company positively in the community. The new strategies of the neighbor of choice shift that role to the general managers of the company. It is their function to establish

Figure 4.4
The Elements of the Factual, Qualitative, and Strategic Information for a
Company Assessment

Factual	Qualitative	Strategic
Contributions	Willingness to plan	Strengths
Volunteerism	Relationships in	Company
Partnerships	community	Community relations
Policies	Community needs,	Weaknesses
	attitudes, and	Company
	expectations	Community relations

trusting relationships in the community. It is their function to make the decisions as to which community programs are needed to support company strategies and goals.

For some community relations managers, this is a challenge. It will require them to learn new responsibilities, to learn how to work through general managers to facilitate their ability to carry out community relations functions. Some community relations managers have the temperament, personality, and knowledge to function as coaches or as members of management teams. Others do not. The need to explore these weaknesses is necessary for the design of neighbor of choice strategies.

The strategic information in the internal assessment is designed to define the strengths and weaknesses of the company's community reputation and programs and the strengths and weaknesses of the company's community relations program (see Figure 4.4). The strategic assessment is a necessary premise for designing the neighbor of choice strategies. The company's external affairs officers should be responsible for conducting the strategic assessment. It is an activity that should be conducted every three to four years and whenever there is a review of strategy.

SUMMARY

The internal assessment is the beginning step in the information or data-gathering process for designing strategies to implement the neighbor of choice principle. Three categories of information are needed. One is factual information about current contributions, volunteers, and partnership programs with community organizations. In addition, a summary of the policies governing the community relations programs and actions is also compiled.

A second category of information is qualitative in nature. It is the assessment of the relationships the company has with community organizations, manager and employee perceptions of the company's reputation, community needs of employees, and a statement of the expectations the company has for the community along with a perception of what the community expects from the company. Included in the qualitative assessment is an assessment of the CEO and senior managers' willingness and readiness to engage in redesigning and reengineering the company's community relations strategies.

The third category of information needed is strategic in scope. It is an assessment of the company's strengths and weaknesses, including the strengths and weaknesses of community relations activities and programs.

NOTES

1. H. Mintzberg, "The Fall and Rise of Strategic Planning," *Harvard Business Review*, January–February 1994, p. 109.

2. Ann Pomykal, interview with author, Santa Barbara, CA, March 16, 1998.

3. Kathy Carey, interview with author, Santa Barbara, CA, March 16, 1998.

4. Ashley DesMartens, interview with author, San Diego, CA, January 30, 1997.

5. M. Langley, "Gift Rift: High-Tech Companies Battle over the Value of Donated Software," *Wall Street Journal*, September 9, 1997, pp. A1, A10.

6. H. Rothermand, letter to author, June 16, 1997.

7. J. B. Quinn, *Strategies for Change: Logical Incrementalism* (Homewood, IL: Irwin, 1980). See also H. Mintzbergh, *The Rise and Fall of Strategic Planning* (New York: Free Press, 1994), pp. 108–109; A. C. Hax and N. S. Majluf, *The Strategy Concept and Process: A Pragmatic Approach* (Englewood Cliffs, NJ: Prentice-Hall, 1996), p. 22.

8. Research and Forecasts, *The Chivas Regal Report on Working Americans: Emerging Values for the 1990s* (New York: House of Seagram, 1989); R. Barnes, *Measurement of Consumer Reaction to Socially Responsible Companies*: A Research Report from The Center for Corporate Community Relations at Boston College, 1994 (Chestnut Hill, MA: The Center for Corporate Community Relations at Boston College, 1994).

Chapter 5

Who Are the
Company's Communities?

The second step in implementing the neighbor of choice principle, or any of its selected strategies, is the external, or community assessment. Similar to the internal assessment, there are three categories of information to be collected. Factual information is one category. Information on a community's demography, its needs, and its political structure is an example. The second is qualitative information: What, for example, is the reputation of the company in the community? And the third is strategic: What opportunities exist and what threats confront the company in the community?

The community, however, is a much more complex environment than the company. The way decisions are made and influenced in a community, for example, differs widely from the way they are made in a company. A great many more people become involved in community decision making; some are charged with the responsibility for making decisions, whereas others have no authority except their ability to persuade others to agree with them.

The process itself is also complex. It involves interactions among a number of different individuals and groups. There are also rituals and rules that have to be observed. Those who violate the rules, even inadvertently, pay penalties.

Communities, as I pointed out in Chapter 1, have deep meanings for people. They are not just places where people reside. They are sources of comfort, security, and friendships. Communities are often idealized. People, therefore, strive to protect and preserve their idealized notion of *their* community.

Second, there are many different types of communities to which companies must respond even within a geographically designated political subdivision.[1] It is inadequate to define the community as a place where a company is located or headquartered. There are, for example, headquarters communities and plant communities. There are also communities in which the company is not located but might be important to the company. Examples would be communities where the employees live or communities adjacent to the company's site affected by the company's operations. Then there are neighborhoods surrounding the plant and communities of common interests that are also different kinds of communities. All of these may have some impact in one way or another on the company.

Moreover, each of these different kinds of communities has the capacity to influence the company in different ways and for different reasons. A neighborhood surrounding a plant may be less interested in contributions to local charities than in the operational practices of the company—noise, smoke, parking, or traffic, for example. On the other hand, residents in the headquarters community may be concerned about the company's support of community services. Plant community residents may be very interested in whether or not the company is going to continue its operations, close down, or move to another community. And some communities may make claims on the resources of the company because of the effect the company's operations may have on the community, even though the company may not be located in the community.

Before an external assessment can be conducted, therefore, a company has to identify the types of communities in which to conduct the assessments. It also has to identify the sources of the information it wants to collect. Who in the community, for example, should be asked about the company's reputation? Or who should be asked about the needs of a community? These premises for conducting an assessment will be the subject of this and the next chapters.

DEFINING THE COMMUNITY

There are six different types of communities—site, employee, fenceline, impact, cyber, and common interest—with which companies may be involved (Figure 5.1). The number of types of communities will differ from one company to the next, depending on the present or potential impact of the company on the community or the impact of the community on the company. The scope and degree of involvement will also differ from one type of company to another. In some communities, a company may need to develop comprehensive programs of relationship building, contributions, and issues identification. But in others, a company may need only to develop programs of relationship building.

The kinds and range of programs will depend on:

Historical relationships

The needs of the community

The impact of the operations of the company on the community

The degree of relationships the company has to establish with the community

The importance of the community to the company's business goals and strategies

Figure 5.1
Types of Communities for Corporate Involvement

Site Community

The *site community* is defined by its geographical boundaries. It is the city or town in which a company and any of its major facilities are located. Some companies may have only one site community, whereas others may have several plants located in communities around the world. Then, too, utilities have many site communities within their service areas.

The site community is an important and influential community. It is the major definer of the company's license or freedom to operate. It may also have historical significance. Some—although fewer and fewer as corporations become more global—are named after the community in which their headquarters are located—Pittsburgh Plate and Glass, Marion (Ohio) Power Shovel Company, Cincinnati Bell Telephone Company, and BankBoston. Neither was it uncommon for companies to name a production facility after the community even if the headquarters was elsewhere. The jet engine facility of General Electric Company in Lynn, Massachusetts, for example, is called the "Lynn Works." The "Homestead Works" was a plant operated by the former U.S. Steel Company in Pittsburgh.

The site community enacts laws and regulations that determine how and where the company can operate in the community. It also imposes taxes on the company as a cost of operating in the community. In return, the community provides services to the company—fire, safety, education, transportation, and the like.

The site community has its own growing set of behavioral expectations—

support of local charities, sensitivity to environmental concerns, respect for cultural traditions, and involvement in community problem solving, for example. Other community expectations may include increasing minority representation in a company, purchasing from minority-owned companies, and supporting local small businesses. These are part of the unwritten expectations, described earlier as part of the psychological contract, that communities have for companies.

A company's headquarters community may have a unique set of expectations greater and apart from the expectations that a community has for a company's plant or facilities communities. Communities believe that companies headquartered in their town owe a special obligation to that community. Traditionally, this expectation has been honored. Companies have been more generous and more involved in headquarters communities, although this, too, is changing.

As companies become more global and as ownership of companies begins to be assumed by companies in communities quite distant and, in a growing number of cases, in other countries, this unique relationship, however, becomes difficult to maintain. Loyalties shift. As communities around the world begin to insist that companies assume more responsibility in the communities in which they operate, then the demands of these communities and former headquarters communities will come into conflict.

Pillsbury, for example, a mainstay of Minneapolis, is owned by Diageo, P.L.C. (formerly Grand Metropolitan), a company located in London. The chairman and CEO of Diageo, Allen Sheppard, has been a longtime supporter of Business in the Community (BITC) in the United Kingdom. He served as chair of BITC from 1996 to 1997 and contributed generously to the organization.

This is an emerging challenge. Companies are going to have to find ways to balance these kinds of arrangements and loyalties among their facilities and site communities.

Employee Community

The *employee community* is not the employees as a community but is composed of those communities outside the site community where many company employees may live. In order to attract and retain employees, companies need to be concerned about the quality of life in all the communities where their employees live. Moreover, employees often want the company to support programs and services in the communities in which they live and believe the company has an obligation to do so. Employees rarely make a distinction between the site community and the community in which they live when it comes to the company's philanthropy. Furthermore, employees are engaged in volunteer activities in the communities in which they live and, consequently, are invested in their communities. They expect the company to be equally invested.

It is also not uncommon for community-based organizations to expect support from their residents' employers. Local United Ways have made this claim for years as a rationale for corporate contributions from companies outside the home city of the United Way agency. In fact, many pledge cards for United Way now provide an option for employees to donate to a United Way in their residence community.

Fenceline Community

The *fenceline community* is made up of the immediate neighbors surrounding the property of a company. The residents of the fenceline community are impacted directly by the operations of the company: Noise, parking, traffic, odors, and even employee behavior have an influence on the neighbors adjacent to the company's operations.

Companies are affected by the fenceline community in different and varying degrees. For manufacturing, chemical, pharmaceutical, sports, entertainment, colleges and universities, and retail companies, for example, the fenceline community is critically important. Fenceline residents can exert considerable influence on the operations of the company far beyond the neighborhood boundaries. A fenceline community can use its influence to determine whether or not the company can expand or conduct specific operations, and possibly its hours of operation.

It may, in fact, decide if the company can operate at all. In Lodi, New Jersey, a paint company that had a fire was unable to rebuild because of pressures from the fenceline community. Fordham University, as was pointed out earlier, had considerable difficulty involving costly delays in building a radio tower because of the objections of its fenceline neighbor, the New York Botanical Garden.

Fenceline communities may not exist for some companies. Neighbors of financial institutions and corporate offices of companies located in a downtown office building, for example, are rarely significantly impacted or negatively affected by a company. Hotels and retail establishments in *urban* areas may be other examples.

Impact Community

Some business decisions or business operations can affect a community even though the company is not located in that community. Examples can include transporting materials through a community or discharging effluents in an adjacent community. These are called *impact communities*. There are four different kinds of impact communities.

One, called *operations impact*, is a community outside the site and employee communities that is affected by the operations of the company. A vivid example is a community impacted by a company's discharge of waste into a stream or river. Another example is Shell U.K., which was cited in the introduction. Its decision to dispose of the oil rig in the North Atlantic had an impact on communities in the United Kingdom and Germany. Other examples include airports, railroads, and trucking companies whose operations may affect many communities.

A second kind of impact community is an *influence impact* community. These are communities in which the company chooses to have an impact. It wants to influence certain segments of a community in which it is not located. A capital city is one example. Polaroid Corporation, for example, is headquartered in Cambridge, Massachusetts, but it wants to have an influence in the adjacent capital city, Boston. While the bulk of its community relations activities take place in Cambridge or in plant site communities, it also conducts community programs, makes corporate grants, and maintains relationships with key stakeholders in Boston for that reason.

A third impact community, called an *exiting impact* community, is one from which a company is moving. To lessen the impact of its move, the company decides that it will continue to support local organizations, at least for a specific period of time. Merck, for example, agreed to continue its level of funding to the public school system when it moved its headquarters out of Rahway, New Jersey. Stride Rite made a commitment to continue supporting organizations on a decreasing basis in Cambridge, Massachusetts, when it moved its operations to a community west of Cambridge. When it announced that it was closing plants in eight communities, Levi Strauss pledged $8 million over a three-year period to community groups and organizations in each of the communities.[2]

Sometimes such support is forced on a company. When the Cleveland Browns moved to Baltimore, the city obtained a commitment from the National Football League and the Browns' organization to contribute to the building of a new stadium. Maytag was required to pay 800 workers $11.5 million in compensation when it abruptly decided to move a plant out of Ranson, West Virginia.

An *entry* community is the fourth type of impact community. When a community is selected as a possible future site, whether publicly announced or not, it becomes an *entry impact* community. Before a company moves into a community, there are all sorts of permitting requirements. Engineers, environmental specialists, real estate people, government affairs staffs, and public relations staffs are often involved.

Community relations functions need to be integral to such a move. One example cited earlier is the preparation made by Merck when it moved its headquarters to Whitehouse Station in New Jersey. The fact that the communtiy relations manager was in the community two years in advance of the move helped Merck make design changes in order to comply with neighbors' requests.

Before it moved a semiconductor manufacturing facility into Goochland County, Virginia, Motorola used its Web site to announce its intentions to be a respected corporate neighbor. It described its community relations practices and programs in other cities. It also provided an 800 telephone number to answer any questions from area residents.

Cyber Community

The fifth type of community is one that is very new for companies. Called the *cyber community*, it shares very little of the characteristics of the other communities. It does not have the usual boundaries that other communities have, nor does it exhibit the decision-making characteristics of other communities. There is no leadership pattern or structure.

Yet it is an emerging community. One writer calls it the city of bits.[3] An article in the *Harvard Business Review* advises companies to establish electronic communities on the Internet to provide information, market and sell products, and develop a *community of interest*.[4]

Many companies use the Internet to describe their community relations programs. Web pages of companies such as AT&T, Silicon Graphics, IBM, and Sun Microsystems have been developed to describe the company's community programs and its contributions guidelines. Grant applications are also listed on the Web page.

Of major importance to companies is the use that activist groups are making of the Internet to publicize and comment on corporate practices. Greenpeace, for example, set up a home page on the Brent Spar decision and made extensive use of the Internet to garner support for its successful opposition of Shell's disposal of a used oil rig in the North Atlantic. The Sierra Club offers ten tips for boycotting an oil company on its Web pages. The Net, according to a *Business Week* article, was instrumental in the recall of Dodge Caravan minivans in April because of a grassroots effort begun by a consumer.[5]

Environmentalists in one country, according to Thomas Friedman, the foreign affairs columnist for the *New York Times*, are using the Internet to quickly relay how a company behaves environmentally in other countries, and these can either open doors or close them. "There is no hiding place," says one activist quoted by Friedman, "anymore for bad corporate behavior in a world of globally interconnected activism."[6]

Common Interest Communities

A sixth type of community is called a *common interest community*. Common interest communities were first identified by sociologist Murray Ross, describing a theory of community organization practice for community planners. He called them "functional communities."

For community planning purposes, there are two types of communities, according to Ross. One is the geographical community—that is, people living in a geographical area: neighborhood, city, region, state, or country. These are what I have termed *site communities*. The second is organized groups of people who share some common interest or function, such as environment, education, welfare, religion, or ethnicity. These are what Ross called *functional communities*.[7]

Although the term has changed, the concepts developed by Ross still guide the social work practice of community organization.[8]

It is not uncommon to refer to such groupings as communities: for example, the "environment" community, the "health" community, the "education" community, the "religious" community, the "ethnic" community. Some common interest communities may be even further subdivided: for example, the "Hispanic" community, the "African-American" community, the "Italian" community, or the "disabled" community.

The purpose of a common interest community is to bring together all those who share an interest in common, develop plans that meet the needs of the common interest community, and win support for the plans from the larger or geographic community. The disabled community is a good example. As a common interest community, it is composed of many individuals—some disabled, some not—and groups who share a goal to meet the needs of the disabled. The goal is to convince the larger geographic community to accept its plans and programs.

Common interest communities should not be confused with special interest groups. Common interest communities are made up of all or many of the individuals and groups who are interested in a particular interest or function, including special interest groups. Within the disabled community, for example, are more specialized groups—hearing impaired, mentally ill, substance abuse groups, for example, each with their own agenda. They help to define the larger agenda of the disabled community. And they are able to use the interests of the common interest community to gain their individual ends. The federal and state programs to support education for the handicapped emerged originally from the early work of parents of the mentally retarded. By including other handicapped groups, parent groups gathered even more adherents to their cause, which in turn was a powerful force for convincing federal and state governments (the representatives of the geographical community) to adopt legislation supporting education for all the handicapped.

Similar to geographical communities, common interest communities contain formal leaders and informal leaders. Education is a good example. The formal leaders would include the superintendent of schools, elected PTA president, school board, and elected officials who have an oversight responsibility, such as the mayor or city council members. Informal leaders would include business executives, religious leaders, teachers, children's disability organizations, and unions, to name a few.

The decision-making behavior of common interest communities is similar to that of other types of communities. Democratic processes are frequently used to elect leaders and to make decisions. Many common interest communities, even those that are federations of special interest groups, have bylaws and constitutions that describe the organization and the way it operates. Decision making is complex, sometimes involving many individuals, groups, and organizations interacting with one another in attempts to influence a decision or the outcome of an issue—which is the way decisions are made in geographical communities, as city planners have discovered.[9]

SUMMARY

Before a company can conduct an external assessment, it first has to identify the kinds of communities in which to conduct the assessments. We have identified six major types of communities: site, employee, fenceline, impact, cyber, and common interest.

The next step is to identify the sources in a community from whom to obtain the information for the assessment. That is the subject of the next chapter.

NOTES

1. S. A. Waddock and M. E. Boyle, "The Dynamics of Change in Corporate Community Relations," *California Management Review*, Vol. 37, no. 4 (Summer 1995), p. 134.

2. D. D. Johnson, "At Levi Strauss a Big Cutback with Largess," *New York Times*, November 4, 1997, pp. D1, D26.

3. W. J. Mitchell, *City of Bits* (Cambridge, MA: MIT Press, 1995).

4. A. Armstrong and F. Hagel III, "The Real Value of On-Line Communities," *Harvard Business Review*, May–June 1996, pp. 134–141.

5. "Consumers Unite Community," *Business Week*, July 1, 1996, p. 6.

6. T. L. Friedman, "Surfing the Wetlands," *New York Times*, August 1, 1998, p. 27A.

7. M. G. Ross, *Community Organization: Theory and Principles* (New York: Harper & Row Publishers, 1955), pp. 40–41. See also R. Warren, *The Community in America*, 3rd ed. (Chicago: Rand McNally College Publishing Company, 1978).

8. See, for example, H. Abatema, "The Significance of Planned Community Participation in Problem Solving and Developing a Viable Community Capability," *Journal of Community Practice*, Vol. 42, no. 2 (1997), pp. 13–34; B. Checkoway, "Core Concepts of Community Change," *Journal of Community Practice*, Vol. 4, no. 1 (1997), pp. 11–30; L. Taaffe and R. Fisher, "Public Life in Gulfton: Multiple Publics and Models of Community Organization," *Journal of Community Practice*, Vol. 4, no. 1 (1997), pp. 31–56.

9. See E. C. Banfield, *Political Influence* (New York: Free Press, 1965), and A. Altshuler, *The City Planning Process* (New York: Cornell University Press, 1964), for examples.

Chapter 6

The "Shadow Constituencies"

In the fall of 1959 a sports reporter for *The Repository*, Canton, Ohio's local newspaper, proposed to Clayton Horn, the paper's publisher, that a football hall of fame should be built in their town. It certainly was appropriate. Canton was the home of the nation's first professional football team—the Canton Bulldogs. Horn, reported to be one of the ten most influential people in the county at the time, thought it was a great idea. He recruited William Unstaadt, president of the Timken Company, and Paul Brown, owner of the Cleveland Browns, to spearhead the effort.

Unstaadt headed up a community fund-raising drive and got the support of the business community. Brown handled relationships with the National Football League. Horn took care of publicity. On December 9, 1959, the campaign began with a story in *The Repository* headlined "Pro Football Needs Hall of Fame and Logical Site Is Here." Some $400,000 was raised from the community in nine weeks. The Timken Company gave $100,000. The city donated the land on a continuing lease of $1 a year. In two years it was built.[1]

This is the way projects were completed in most American communities. Community decisions were confined to a few issues, and the way they were made was simple and uncomplicated. Someone in authority or influence had an idea, proposed a course of action, recruited a few friends, and implemented the decision.

The decisions were the result of the interactions of a small group of formal (public officials) and informal influentials in a community.[2] Called a "power structure" by researchers, the process was described as a pyramid composed of four different tiers of influence. Business executives, no more than seven to eight, composed the top tier, followed by bank vice presidents, small business owners, top public officials, and corporate attorneys. Civic organization person-

nel, newspaper columnists, civic agency board members, lower-level public officials, ministers, teachers, and social workers rounded out the bottom two tiers.

Each tier had its own function and role. Business executives viewed their role
as community leaders using their power to influence public opinion and determine community policy. Each of the other tiers was involved in some aspect of
carrying out the policy of the business leaders. It was not uncommon, however,
for someone from the lower tiers to suggest a policy initiative. Without the
sanction of the top tier, however, it was unlikely that the policy would be accepted, let alone implemented.[3]

And the way the decisions were made reflected community expectations. Few
ever questioned a business leader taking responsibility for determining the needs
of a community. There was a belief that those in "authority" were acting in
the best interests of the community.

It is highly doubtful that in all but probably a few rural communities the
process works that way today. For one thing, there is much more involvement
and participation of the public in community issues and affairs than there was
prior to the 1960s. Community residents are far more sophisticated about community issues and how to go about influencing decisions. Moreover, they are
much more skillful in using the media and in community organizing techniques
learned in the civil rights movement and honed in the citizen participation programs of the federal urban renewal and antipoverty initiatives of the 1960s and
1970s. They become "shadow constituencies," which companies, says Lloyd
Dennis, a senior public affairs official with the Los Angeles Water Department,
are foolish to ignore.[4]

Contrast, for example, Canton's experience with the efforts in Boston to build
a new stadium for its professional football team, the New England Patriots. The
need for a stadium was well established. The team played in a poorly built and
obsolete facility in a small southeastern Massachusetts community. Transportation to the stadium was a weekly nightmare. Hotel and other accommodations
for visitors were scarce.

The impetus for the stadium gained momentum when a popular Boston busi-
nessman, Robert Kraft, bought the team, promising to spare no expenses to bring
a championship to New England. He hired Bill Parcells, who had led the New
York Giants to two Super Bowl championships. Parcells brought a succession
of winning Patriots' seasons including a spot in the 1997 Super Bowl. This
turned the team into instant heroes and brought about a groundswell of public
support for a new stadium in Boston.

With the governor's backing, the Port Authority recommended a vacant site
it owned that was adjacent to a sea channel alongside derelict warehouses and
railroad tracks. Located on the edge of working-class South Boston, the site was
connected by all major public transportation facilities and the Massachusetts
Turnpike. It also was next to a proposed convention center and would have been
part of a larger plan to upgrade and improve the area. From practically all
respects, it was an ideal site. An ideal site, that is, except from the neighbor-

hood's point of view. Residents quickly told Kraft that they did not want a football stadium in their neighborhood. It would be disruptive to the neighborhood's quality of life, flood the streets with traffic, and make parking all but impossible.

Just as quickly, they organized a "Sack the Stadium" Committee and mobilized dozens of existing community and neighborhood groups to oppose the stadium plan. Kraft had the support of the governor, some state politicians, trade unions, both Boston newspapers, the influential BankBoston, and sports fans. But he could not win over the neighbors.

This became immediately evident at the first meeting Kraft had with neighborhood leaders and city officials at Boston City Hall on December 19, 1996. An architectural sketch of the proposed stadium, called an "Urban Events Center," was displayed and for nearly two hours Patriots representatives described the proposal and its glowing benefits for the community. The South Boston neighborhood leaders were unswayed. They unanimously voted against the proposal, prompting one city councilor from South Boston to turn to the president of the city council and the state representative from South Boston at the meeting and whisper, "Let's kill this thing now."

Kraft was determined to go forward. He hired lobbyists and public relations firms, met with the governor, the Cardinal, leaders in the state senate and house, federal congressmen and senators, and unions representing construction workers. Over $4 million was spent by Kraft to "sell" his stadium plan in South Boston. He explained the plan in small meetings of selected officials but declined to attend a meeting of residents in a neighborhood school to explain the plan. Thirteen hundred residents showed up on that day, January 9.

On February 21, Kraft bowed to the inevitable and, with popular U.S. Congressman Joseph Moakley at his side, announced he was giving up. Ironically, at the very same time, the South Boston committee was holding its first in a series of planned fund-raising events to support opposition efforts. It turned into a spontaneous victory celebration.[5]

Kraft's experience with the politics of community decision making is not an anomaly. Consider what happened to the Walt Disney Company when it revealed it was opening a 3,000-acre historical theme park in Haymarket, Virginia, four miles from the Manassas National Battlefield Park. In announcing its decision, the Disney Company assured the residents that the benefits to the community would be unsurpassed. It would cost $650 million, bring 12,000 new jobs, and generate $1.68 billion in taxes. In addition, the company promised to manage the growth, maintain the integrity of the area, respect the environment, and establish traffic control procedures.

The company had the support of all county and state officials, including the governor, along with financial incentives from the state to improve the roads. The company also had the wholehearted backing of the Haymarket community.[6] And as I stated earlier, Michael Eisner, chairman and CEO of Disney, agreed to comply with every regulatory requirement—33 local, state, and federal regulations and 72 permits.[7]

Despite the support of the top leaders, Disney was forced to abandon its plans. A local historical society galvanized the support of wealthy residents and historians from the surrounding suburbs, some of whom did not want their privacy to be invaded and others who saw the park as a vulgar intrusion on the environment and historical legacy of the area. Committees were organized; one, the Piedmont Environmental Council, was a coalition of 70 organizations and 5,000 families in northern Virginia. Another, Project Historic America, was composed of what the *Times* called "a veritable pantheon of historians and writers—C. Van Woodward, John Hope Franklin, James McPherson, Shelby Foote, Barbara Fields."[8] The National Trust for Historic Preservation took out an ad opposing the park in the *Washington Post*. Nationally known columnists such as George Will, presidential political advisers, including Mary Matalin and historian David McCullough, along with over 200 historians nationwide rallied to the defense of the little-known county historical society. Environmental lawsuits and other obstacles would have delayed the opening of the park, according to a Disney spokesperson, well beyond the scheduled date in 1998. The decision to scrap the plan was not only prudent but economically necessary.

The governor, state leaders, and community residents of Haymarket were angered and disappointed. The flag in front of city hall flew at half staff for the first time, according to Haymarket's mayor Jack R. Kapp, since Jacqueline Kennedy Onassis died.[9]

INFLUENCES IN THE COMMUNITY

As these examples illustrate, what is different between the 1950s and now is that there are more "players" in the "game" of community decision making and therefore more individuals and groups that can affect a company's license to operate. Moreover, the players or stakeholders are considerably more knowledgeable about how to influence a community decision and the behavior of a company.

Another difference is the distinction between community power and influence. The early studies that found a hierarchy of power composed of a few influential individuals appears to be rare. While it is certainly true that some stakeholders have more power than others by virtue of their position, resources, or characteristics, other stakeholders are able to create or concert a number of resources to influence a community decision or change the behavior of a company.[10] The process itself, moreover, is more complex than it once was. It emerges out of interactions involving a significant number of individual groups and organizations, each vying with one another to influence the outcome of a decision.[11]

While it may appear that it is haphazard, accidental, or irrational—which in fact it may be at times—there is an explainable logic to the process—even a logic to the irrational. Certain norms of practice and even behavior are observed.

It may not necessarily be polite. It may indeed be confrontational, involving angry public meetings, even picketing and boycotts, but these behaviors can sometimes be predictable.

One analyst has likened the process to a game that provides the players with set rules that help the players know how the game should be played. It also provides the players with goals that can explain success and failure. And it also help others who enter into the game to understand their roles and the roles of other players.[12] Consider, for example, in baseball, that when a ground ball is hit to the third baseman, we have certain expectations. We expect the third baseman to field the ball and throw it to the first baseman. Everyone observing the incident has the same expectation. The roles of the game are carried out.

When a company, using the analogy, makes a decision to build or expand a facility, we can expect that some will support the decision, whereas others will oppose it. It is possible to anticipate who these "players" will be. The opposition may be a homeowners' association, environmental groups, community activists, or even a group of neighbors who quickly learn how to organize one another. Supporters may include city officials, real estate groups, leaders of influential organizations, and business leaders. Supporters may also include individuals associated with the company. Employees are an example. But supporters of the company may also include residents who have positive relationships with the company through participation in one of the company's relationship programs or have benefited from a company contribution program. Each may singly or in combination try to influence the acceptance of the decision. How they go about using the influence they have or can concert by organizing can very well determine the eventual decision outcome.

Sometimes there are miscalculations. Those who the company thought would be supporters turn out to be indifferent or at worst outright opponents. But baseball players make errors, too. They work at overcoming errors, however, by training and practicing regularly. The "game" of community decision making also can be learned. There are certain principles that companies such as Merck and Bristol-Myers Squibb are using to train managers how to understand and influence community decision making.

Decision making in communities, as I noted, is dispersed among a number of decision centers, some formally constituted, such as elected and appointed public officials, and some that are informal, such as organizations and groups in communities. The decision making is less a logical series of discrete steps from beginning to end than a process, a series of activities. Some activities may be haphazard or unexplained—capriciousness, reflex actions; some may be routine—habit, standard procedures; whereas others may be purposive and deliberate—reflection, analyses, planning.[13]

Some individuals, we have learned, have more ability to influence decisions than others. These individuals are known as opinion leaders, and there are two kinds. Certainly those with legitimate authority, for example, mayors, superintendents of schools, heads of governmental departments, and executive directors of community-based organizations, are in positions that give them the right and mandate to make decisions. This is the formal leadership function first identified in the early cited community power studies,[14] which is one form of an *influence resource*.

There is a second group of individuals who may not be in positions of formal or legitimate authority but who also have a high degree of community influence. They are in leadership roles with business, professional, and community organizations. These are the people, for example, selected to run the United Way drive, chair the mayor's task force on economic development, or sponsor a testimonial dinner in support of a community charity or any of a number of high-profile community activities. They are able to exert influence through their leadership involvement in community activities or as a consequence of the networking that such activities provide. Moreover, as studies in mass communications reveal, their opinions influence the decisions of others. Consequently, their opinions are widely respected and often sought.

Opinion leaders, or key leaders, as they are sometimes called, do not intervene in all community issues. The decision to intervene is based on a number of considerations, not the least of which is the importance of the issue to the opinion leader. In the New England Patriots' case, the business leaders in Boston refrained from endorsing the site in South Boston or supporting Robert Kraft, one of their colleagues. The issue appeared to be too confrontational, the stakes too high, and the consequences too unpredictable.

Unlike the Canton, Ohio, example, no single group of opinion leaders today has the power to influence all decisions in a community. With perhaps the exception of small rural communities, groups of opinion leaders are organized around specific issues or interests, such as education, economic development, health, welfare, environment, and safety. Individuals active in one issue area are generally not active or opinion leaders in other issue areas. This is only practical. It is difficult for any one person or organization to be involved in all issues in a community. A division of labor around interests appears to occur naturally. Business executives, for example, tend to be active in issues related to the United Way or economic and community development concerns. Health care officials and doctors organize around health issues, environmentalists organize around their concerns, and social workers are involved in children's issues and issues of poverty.

These are not rigid or exclusive boundaries, however. There is considerable crossover and shifting of interests and concerns over time. When Frederick Allen was CEO of Pitney Bowes, he served as director of the Stamford Economic Assistance Corporation and the Connecticut Economic Development Corporation. He is also credited with helping to promote Stamford as a location for corporate headquarters in part by building the company's new headquarters in a depressed area of the city. Allen also served on boards of the local and national United Way. Many business executives have assumed leadership functions in education as a consequence of the inability of public education to prepare students for businesses' technology needs. The Business Roundtable, an organization composed of major company CEOs, for example, organized CEOs in dozens of states to support a large initiative to reform public education.

Such shifts in interest and concern are not confined to business leaders. Superintendents of schools and school board members, for example, became involved in community efforts to reduce crime when schools were engulfed in violence. Similarly, lawyers and judges are active in issues related to women and child abuse.

In addition to legitimate authority and opinion leadership, which are the most powerful, there are other resources used by people and groups that can influence community opinions and decisions.

Money. Money has long been used as a resource to influence decisions. One example: contributions for the purpose of potentially influencing a political official. Money is also a very powerful resource for subsidizing organized campaigns to influence public opinion. The organization, for example, that initiated the campaign to halt Disney's efforts to open the theme park in Virginia received significant contributions of funds from wealthy residents to finance its campaign. In fact, without significant financial support, it is doubtful if the opposition to the park would have succeeded.

Companies have also established and funded their own "community" organizations to support the company's plans and objectives. Called "astro turf" organizations, they have become suspect and ineffectual and frequently backfire.

The *Los Angeles Times* obtained confidential documents revealing plans by Microsoft to commission flattering articles, letters to editors, and opinion pieces to support the company in its fight against antitrust accusations. Embarrassed officials at first denied the report and then had to admit its existence.

Phillip Morris bankrolled an organization called "National Smokers Alliance," a smokers' rights group, to push back antismoking campaigns in state legislatures. Publicity about the astro turf organization and its support by Phillip Morris contributed to the already free-falling reputation of the tobacco industry.[15]

Control over votes. The ability to control votes, as organizations such as the National Rifle Association, the American Association of Retired Persons (AARP), and the Association of Community Organizations for Reform Now (ACORN) have demonstrated, is an effective tool for influencing decisions and the behavior of public officials and organizations. In fact, these organizations depend heavily on their membership base to influence companies and community officials.

Individuals themselves have also discovered the power of organization as a vote-threatening resource to affect decisions. The community residents in South Boston were able to use this as a threat to convince local political officials, including a U.S. congressman and the mayor of Boston, to oppose the stadium.

Persistence. The squeaky wheel. Mothers against Drunk Driving is an example. Along with using other influence resources, such as control over votes, they changed a nation's attitudes about drinking and driving and were even able, despite repeated rebuffs and disappointments including the opposition of President Reagan, to establish 21 as the legal age for alcohol consumption in the United States. MADD refused to give up despite the obstacles.

Another example and one that illustrates the power of one person in influencing decisions is the efforts of a single mother, Anne Marie Mueser, who waged a ten-year battle with the Iroquois Pipeline Operating Company to remove a gas line through her community of Clifton Conners, New York. Her efforts resulted in rerouting the pipeline and in the conviction of the company's former president and other executives for violating the Clean Water Act. The company was fined $22 million, the largest environmental fine since the Exxon *Valdez* incident.[16]

Communication. There are two aspects to the role of communication as an influence resource. One is the communication media, and the other is the growing use of communication technology—faxes, Internet, and so on—to influence opinions and decisions.

Surprisingly, the media has little effect on the specific outcome of a community issue or decision. Even in earlier studies of community power the media was not found in the top tier of power. The media, however, does have a significant role in community decision making, because it can control the public agenda. Its ability to keep an issue alive on the agenda until some action is taken gives the media its clout on community decisions—as public officials and business leaders have all too well discovered, prompting the familiar complaint, "Why do they have to keep harping on that?"

It was the day-to-day, week-to-week reporting of Woodward and Bernstein on Watergate, for example, that eventually brought about President Richard Nixon's resignation. The decision to fine Exxon $5 billion was influenced in great measure by the constant reporting of the *Valdez* accident by the media. It was a drumbeat of constant reporting. In an editorial the *New York Times* excoriated the company, accusing the company of reckless behavior.[17] This in turn encouraged other lawsuits.

But as a consequence of its resource, the press can be unwittingly manipulated. Fenton Communications, for example, successfully used the press in 1989 to focus public attention on the alleged and dubious charge that apples treated with the pesticide Alar could cause cancer in children. Ed Bradley, using an overlay of a skull and crossbones over an apple, introduced the charge on *60 Minutes*. Actress Meryl Streep became a spokesperson for the anti-Alar campaign, appearing at press conferences, once with the national president of the PTA. It was a media-staged strategy. Apple sales plummeted. Growers lost fortunes. Before any correct explanation was possible, Uniroyal, maker of Alar, was forced to take the product off the market.[18]

A second and growing influence resource is the use of communication technology to mobilize action or to publicize an issue. The decade of the 1960s was the birth of advocacy in community politics. Its reemergence in the late 1980s has been distinguished by its success in using communication technology to promote an issue and to galvanize groups into instantaneous action. Greenpeace, as I pointed out earlier, made effective use of the Internet to gain support for its efforts to halt the deepwater disposal of the Shell oil rig, and historians in Virginia used the computer network to organize historians across the country to oppose the Walt Disney Company.

Organization. Organizations play a distinct and unique role in America. Over a century ago, Alexis de Tocqueville noted, "Americans of all ages, all conditions, and all dispositions constantly form associations. Whenever at the head of some new undertaking you see the government in France, or a man of rank in England, in the United States, you will be sure to find an association."[19] This has never been more true than it is today. Since de Tocqueville's time, the number of organizations has increased astronomically.

Organizations have a great influence on our thinking and our actions. Organizations as large as a bureaucratic agency to a small neighborhood tenants association shape the way people inside and outside of these organizations operate. "Organizations," explains Charles Euchner, who has studied the new role of organizations in American society, "do not *determine* [his emphasis] human behavior, but they do give form to people's activity."[20]

Moreover, organized efforts to influence a decision have become a highly effective method in community politics. In fact, studies show that organized efforts to achieve success in implementing a community project are more important than any other influence resource.[21]

Also, Americans have become highly sophisticated in the ability to organize individuals into groups to support a cause or a course of action. In South Boston, for example, a decade-long effort to oppose a court-ordered desegregation effort became a learning curve experience to the football stadium issue. They did not have to start from scratch to organize the opposition. Neither did other community organizations and groups, such as the Mothers against Drunk Driving, community environmentalists, the disabled, and the aged who learned from the civil rights organizing experiences of the 1960s.

In addition, schools have been formed to train professionals in "community organizing." The Industrial Areas Foundation, founded by the late Saul Alinsky, is one of the more famous and effective training grounds for community organizers. Alinsky graduates have successfully brought about community action affecting such companies as Kodak and Allstate Insurance Co.

Schools of social work and public policy schools in universities teach skills and techniques of community organizing. A great many community organizations are staffed by social workers. At one time, community organization taught in schools of social work provided the professional training background for United Way directors.

Friendship networks. Contacts, the ability to know someone in authority or someone who can influence someone in authority, is another way to influence a decision or an opinion. The use of networks or contacts is an old technique in community decision making. The "old boys" network was long used to maintain the influence and power of a few leaders. Now there are many more types of networks, based on profession, personal relationships, ideology, or gender, for example. The use of networks is a resource often used by key opinion leaders.

The ability to enhance a reputation. Some community organizations are able to create and build the reputation of individuals and turn them into figures of authority and consequently influence. The United Way employs this influence resource very effectively by using other United Ways, their national organization, United Way of America, and the media to promote the reputation of its volunteers as community influentials. In turn, of course, this helps to increase the status and reputation of the United Way.

Expertise. Knowledge or information about an issue can be used to influence a decision. The expertise has to be recognized and acknowledged, however. Environmental organizations depend heavily on scientific reports and data to support their initiatives and positions.

Corporations have also hired scientists and university professors as consultants to respond to community questions about a company's environmental practices. Northeast Utilities hired one of its biggest critics to review its safety practices. Oil and chemical companies also encourage employees to volunteer in schools to provide instruction and examples of the value of chemistry and science. The intention is to promote trust and positive attitudes among students about chemical companies.

It is apparent that there are few, if any, people without access to some kind of resource for influencing community decisions and the community decisions that affect companies. As one researcher noted, there are many different resources for influencing decisions, and the resources are available to different citizens. With few exceptions the resources for influencing community decisions are unequally distributed. But most important, "virtually no one, and certainly no group of more than a few individuals is entirely lacking in some influence resource."[22] This is an often neglected lesson of community decision making— the lesson that the Walt Disney Company, the New England Patriots, and the Iroquois Pipeline Company have learned the hard and expensive way.

SUMMARY

Understanding how decisions that affect companies are made in communities is essential for developing strategies and programs to implement the neighbor of choice principle. It is the decisions and influence of individuals in communities that affect a company's license to operate. Moreover, understanding provides the information for identifying key individuals in a community whose opinions are needed for framing operational decisions. Strategies and tactics to enhance or maintain a company's license to operate, therefore, must be based on knowing how community opinions are formed and how decisions are made.

While it is complicated, the process of community decision making in communities is knowable and in many cases predictable. The process often involves the interaction of individuals and groups, each trying to influence an outcome or decision.

People in positions of authority and those who are opinion leaders are the most influential, if they choose to do so, in being able to influence a decision. Nonetheless, a variety of other resources can be used singly or in combination to influence opinions and community decisions. Individuals and groups have discovered how to develop and concert influence to affect community decisions. None should be neglected in framing responses to community issues and, more important, in developing a neighbor of choice strategy.

NOTES

1. M. Winerip, "At 'President McKinley's Paper' the Editors Take Endorsements Seriously," *New York Times*. November 2, 1996, p. 7; telephone conversation with John Bankert, executive director, Football Hall of Fame, March 18, 1996.

2. F. Hunter, *Community Power Structure* (Chapel Hill: University of North Carolina Press, 1953), p. 109.

3. Ibid., pp. 172–174.

4. R. R. Man and L. B. Dennis, "Companies Ignore Shadow Constituencies at Their Peril," *Public Relations Journal*, May 1994, pp. 10–11.

5. T. Cassidy, "Kraft Gives Up on Site," *Boston Globe*, February 22, 1997, pp. A1, A6; C. M. Sennott and T. Cassidy, "How Kraft's Grand Plan Unravelled," *Boston Globe*, February 23, 1997, pp. A1, A24.

6. "Disney Retreats at Bull Run," *New York Times*, September 30, 1994, p. A30.

7. Disney's Virginia Park Will Bring American Experience to Life," *New York Times*, June 23, 1994, p. A26.

8. Rebellion Against Disney," *New York Times*, June 16, 1994, sec. 4, p. 16.

9. Disney Vows to Seek Another Park Site," *New York Times*, September 30, 1994.

10. C. Banfield, *Political Influence* (New York: Free Press, 1965).

11. E. M. Burke, *A Participatory Approach to Urban Planning* (New York: Human Sciences Press, 1979), p. 27.

12. N. Long, "The Local Community as an Ecology of Games," *American Journal of Sociology*, Vol. 64, no. 3 (November 1968), pp. 251–261.

13. Burke, *A Participatory Approach*, p. 45.

14. Hunter, *Community Power Structure*.

15. F. Rich, "Up in Smoke," *New York Times*, April 14, 1998, p. A51.

16. W. Glaberson, "She Pushed for 10 Years and the Pipeline Moved," *New York Times*, June 4, 1996, pp. B1, B6.

17. Editorial, "Long Shadow of the Exxon *Valdez*," *New York Times*, September 21, 1994, p. A22.

18. L. Susskind and P. Field, *Dealing with an Angry Public* (New York: Free Press, 1996), pp. 117, 201.

19. A. de Tocqueville, *Democracy in America* (New York: Alfred A. Knopf, 1945), p. 106.

20. C. C. Euchner, *Extraordinary Politics: How Protest and Dissent Are Changing American Democracy* (Boulder, CO: Westview Press, 1996), p. 110.

21. W. A. Gamson, "Reputation and Resources in Community Politics," *American Journal of Sociology*, Vol. 72, no. 2 (September 1966), pp. 121–131.

22. R. Dahl, *Who Governs?* (New Haven, CT: Yale University Press, 1961), p. 228. See also Burke, *A Participatory Approach*, pp. 25–41.

Chapter 7

The Community Assessment

The community assessment, or as it is sometimes called by strategic planners, the external assessment, is similar in many respects to the company assessment. The intention is to collect information for developing strategies, programs, policies, and procedures that will position the company favorably in the community—or, in other words, to enhance the reputation of the company as a neighbor of choice—and, if the company chooses to do so, contribute to its competitive advantage.

Similar to the company assessment, there are three categories of information needed for the community assessment. One is factual data, which describes the community and its needs. The second is qualitative information, which is an assessment of the community's attitudes to the company. And the third is strategic information, which identifies the community threats and opportunities to the company.

A community assessment should be guided by two questions: What kind of information does the company need? Where and from whom does the company get the information?

KINDS OF INFORMATION

Factual Information

There are four types of factual information that should be gathered in conducting a community assessment. One is community data, the second is information on needs in the community, the third is information on the quality of the community's social and educational resources, and the fourth is information on the community involvement programs of other companies.

Community data. Information on the demographics and the financial condition of the community is one kind of factual data. Other kinds of information that can be helpful include statistics on quality-of-life indicators of the community—crime rates, education reports, employment levels, and the like. Some companies compile historical and cultural information as well as future plans and goals of the community.

This information can be obtained from census reports, planning reports, annual reports of government and private agencies, and reports of studies conducted by community organizations.

Community needs. A second type of factual information is community needs. Needs are expressions of wants or desires. They are also measures of a person's satisfaction with the community in which they live. People want to live and work in communities that have a favorable quality of life. The quality of a community's services—education, health, safety, recreation, for example—often is the principal reason for choosing to live in a specific community.

Companies, consequently, have to be concerned about a community's quality of life. There are, therefore, business reasons why a company would consider conducting a community needs assessment. For one thing, it affects the ability to recruit and retain employees. When Procter & Gamble, for example, was moving into a Florida community, it conducted a needs assessment study and discovered a lack of recreational facilities. Convinced that this would be an obstacle to recruiting the kind of employees it needed, it entered into a partnership with the community. Procter & Gamble would finance building the recreational facilities and the community would provide continuing operating expenses.

A company also depends on other services in a community for which it pays taxes such as fire, safety, and transportation. Assessing the adequacy of services for which it pays taxes is another business reason.

A third reason for conducting a needs assessment is for making decisions on allocating dollars and employees to community services. Contributions decisions, which in the past may have been based on whimsy or the "old boys" network, have to be based today on as much factual information as possible. Contributions budgets have become too significant an expenditure to leave to the personal wishes of a CEO. As a result, periodic needs assessments have become a regular function in many corporations. IBM, Glaxo-Wellcome, Boeing, and Johnson & Johnson are but a few examples of companies that conduct community needs assessments.

A community needs assessment is a method of interviewing community residents or a sample of residents through written surveys or personal interviews to obtain their opinions on the adequacy and relative importance of the needs or problems in a community. The surveys and interviews can be conducted by the company or consultants. The company can also use secondary sources such as the results of needs assessments conducted by other organizations in the community to obtain this information.

There are problems and issues that a company has to consider in using a needs assessment for information to make contributions decisions. Needs, for one thing, are not static or constant. They change and may increase in number and intensity. In fact, the definition of community needs is relative, and according to one federal expert, this is one of the major sources of confusion in conducting community needs assessments.[1] Needs are defined personally and reflect the perspective of the person being interviewed, not the perspective of the total community.

Attempting to determine the relative priority of needs in a community is also problematic. A needs assessment survey reveals only the respondents' perception of need and its priority at the time the needs assessment is conducted. Respondents, for example, may rank housing or education or unemployment in that order as major community needs or problems. If an incident occurs, however, that becomes widely reported in the media—say, for example, a rash of robberies accompanied by brutal murders—then crime becomes *the* major problem. After the O. J. Simpson trial in Los Angeles in 1996, spousal abuse rose to the top of the list as a major national concern. The Louise Woodward trial in Cambridge, Massachusetts, in November 1997 shifted the focus to the problems of working mothers and child abuse. The results of any needs assessment survey are time limited and consequently ephemeral.

A needs assessment, therefore, reveals only the importance of a need or problem at the time of the survey, and it reflects a personal preference or perspective. To offset these problems, companies generally rely on needs assessment reports conducted by other organizations as comparisons. And most important, they rely on the assessment of needs from operating managers and rank-and-file employees.

To guard against a misinterpretation or raising of unrealistic expectations, an interview is often prefaced by the statement that the needs assessment is just one of the means that will be used to make contributions and community relations decisions.

Other companies' programs. A third element in the factual category of a community needs assessment is knowing what other companies are doing. This information is useful to avoid duplication of efforts. At the same time, it may also reveal opportunities to jointly sponsor a program, thereby enhancing and enlarging the scope of a company's own community programs.

A company's community relations manager is the source of this type of information. Community relations managers customarily participate in local networks of other managers, as well as attending and participating in conferences, seminars, and meetings of professional organizations such as the Boston College Center for Corporate Community Relations, the Public Affairs Council, the Conference Board, and the Council on Foundations.

Community resources. The final element of information is the availability and, if possible, the adequacy of the resources in a community established to respond

Figure 7.1
The Elements of the Factual Information for a Community Assessment

---

Factual
Community data
Community needs
Other companies' programs
Community resources

---

to community needs. Companies should compile a list of the major agencies and organizations that influence the community's quality of life.

It is often difficult to obtain information on the adequacy and effectiveness of the community resources. The local United Way is a source of information on the community's social services. United Way of America, the national organization of United Ways, has initiated a program of agency evaluation called *Focus on Program Outcomes: Survey Guide*.[2] Copies of the report can be obtained from United Way of America. National and state associations and organizations in such service areas as education and environment can be a source of evaluative information on these resources. On the whole, data and reports on services and programs in a community are seriously wanting.

Because of the need and importance of service program evaluation, companies have begun to insist on their own evaluation process. The Hitachi Foundation, for example, now requires an evaluation of its grants. Mitsubishi Electric America Foundation published a manual based on its procedures that it has made available for nonprofits. It is a guide useful for companies and nonprofits.[3] Cinergy, an energy company in Cincinnati, uses an unusual method to evaluate its grants and the programs of nonprofit organizations. It makes unannounced site visits, which can include the company's president, to organizations receiving its grants. The president reported that he uses site visits as a means of assuring that the company's grants are being used for their stated purpose.[4]

In summary, there are four elements in the factual category of a community assessment: community data, community needs, other company programs, and the availability of community resources (Figure 7.1).

Qualitative Information

Qualitative information focuses on perceptions and attitudes. It reflects what people are thinking about the company, particularly about its operations and actions. Qualitative information is used primarily to design plans and programs that build sustainable trust in a community.

The elements that are assessed in the qualitative category are:

Concerns
Community expectations

Extent and quality of relationships with key individuals and organizations

Company's reputation

Concerns. Identifying the concerns about the company in the community is important because they often give clues as to how the community expects the company to behave. Is the company honest, fair, and responsible when interacting with community groups and officials? Do the operations of the company—noise, odors, traffic patterns, employees, for example—adversely affect residents in the community, particularly those immediately surrounding the facility, the fenceline community?

Without this information, incidents can fester and later turn into issues weakening the company's freedom to operate. Studies report that companies that take voluntary steps to address community concerns are often spared rigid and costly legislative or regulatory consequences. They are, moreover, in a much better position to generate community goodwill and trust.

Johnson & Johnson's reaction to the Tylenol-tamper scare is often cited as an example of a timely and successful response to an underlying concern of consumers toward a product. Contrary to government agency recommendations, Johnson & Johnson removed all products from store shelves and restored consumer confidence, not just in Tylenol but in its other products as well. Its decisive action enhanced its public image.[5]

Expectations. Assessing expectations is necessary because they form the community's understanding of the contract between it and the company. They are also the basis for judging or taking action for or against a company. If the community, or significant community stakeholders, believes that a company has violated its expectation, it may take punitive action.

Community groups often monitor company performance based on how they expect the company to behave. Banks in Atlanta, Boston, and Detroit, for example, were fined millions of dollars for lending violations uncovered by the Association of Community Organization for Reform Now (ACORN).[6] In other instances, community groups have forced expense delays on company expansions because of expectations over environmental performance.

Moreover, expectations—most important, the implicit expectations—form the basis of the psychological contract between the company and the community. As I will explain in the next chapter, conflicting expectations can be the cause of reducing trust in a company. Before a negotiation can take place, however, the expectations must be uncovered, which is the reason for including expectations in the community assessment.

Relationships. The purpose of assessing relationships is to gauge the scope and, if possible, the quality of relationships the company's managers have with key community individuals. It is important to determine if the range of relationships extends broadly among a broad range of individuals and groups. One measure of relationships is the participation of senior managers in community organizations. To ensure a broad range of participation, some companies make it a practice to refer managers to volunteer in specific community organizations. The manager of community affairs for IBM in the Boston area, for example, made it a practice to interview incoming managers to determine their volunteer interests. If it appeared that the manager wanted to volunteer in an organization that was overly represented by IBM managers, he would suggest, but never insist, other volunteer activities. The interview was also used to relate the volunteer activity with the manager's personnel development needs.

Determining the quality of the relationships the company has with key individuals is frequently difficult to assess. Some of this information can be obtained from the company assessment as described in Chapter 4. Some can also be obtained when conducting a community needs assessment. Although the main purpose of the needs assessment is to identify problems and issues in a community, as described below, it can be used to gather information that is qualitative in scope. It is not uncommon, therefore, for questions in a needs assessment to be used to probe for this kind of information.

In 1994, Glaxo (now Glaxo-Wellcome) conducted a community needs assessment as part of an overall assessment of the company's position in the Raleigh-Durham research triangle area.[7] Key leaders were asked a series of questions that helped to evaluate the company's presence in the community. One question, for example, asked, "What do you think is the most valuable contribution Glaxo has made to our community in the past 5 years?" Another question asked: "What community involvement activities do you think senior executives at Glaxo should be involved in?"

Both questions revealed that the company had a reputation for leadership involvement in the community. Managers were involved in the leading agencies and organizations in the research triangle area. Suggestions for broadening the involvement of the company in child care and school dropout issues were also made by the community's key leaders. The answers enabled the company to reexamine its relationship programs.

Reputation. A fourth element of the qualitative assessment is the reputation of the company in the community. There is increasing recognition that a company's reputation is one of its most important intangible assets. It not only helps to sell products or services, but it is also used to attract employees and investors. Charles Fombrun, a research professor of management at New York University's Stern School of Management, insists that a company's reputation has become a more enduring source of competitive advantage than patents and technologies.[8]

Levi Strauss & Co. engaged all its senior managers in conducting a global reputation audit including an audit of its *community* reputation. Corporate reputation, as defined by Levi Strauss, is the "sustained perception people have of [our] company based on their direct and indirect knowledge or experience with its products, policies, services and/or performance." Reputation is a global asset and, if managed properly, according to the company, can be a competitive advantage.[9]

This is what other companies, benchmarked by Levi Strauss, had to say about reputation:

> The name of our company is the same as our primary product so our corporate and brand reputation can rise and fall together.
>
> —L'Oreal

> Consumers have a tendency to avoid products of companies they dislike.
>
> —Nestlé

> Public confidence is everything.
>
> —Hong Kong and Shanghai Bank

> Our most important activity is product design. Our chairman, Morita-San, believes corporate reputation is the same as product design.
>
> —Sony

> If you're not managing your corporate reputation, you're wasting a global corporate asset.
>
> —Merck

Community reputation is a critical part of assessing the company's global reputation, explains Levi Strauss. To build a reputation, you need to assess it among the key individuals and groups in a community. The reputation assessment is an audit that should be conducted regularly. It should include the perspective not only of customers, investors, and employees but also of the community. The audit should be a "diagnostic review of the company's current identity, images, and reputation."[10]

This type of information can be obtained separately as part of a reputation study, or it can be included as part of a needs assessment study. In the Glaxo study cited earlier, the company conducted what it called a "Counterparts" survey to assess its reputation in the community among eight other companies in the research triangle area. This helped to gauge the company's comparative reputation and identified areas needing improvement.

The qualitative category of the community assessment, as depicted in Figure 7.2, contains information on concerns in the community, community expectations, and community reputation.

Strategic Information

The third category of information needed for the community assessment is strategic in scope. Strategic information focuses on two areas: the opportunities and threats in the community toward the company.

Some of this information can be obtained from the factual and qualitative assessments. Interviews or surveys of managers along with community repre-

Figure 7.2
The Elements of the Factual and Qualitative Information for a Community Assessment

Factual	Qualitative
Community data	Community attitudes,
Community needs	concerns, and
Other companies'	expectations
programs	Company's community
Community resources	reputation

sentatives can point out threats to the company. Identifying opportunities, however, is often a separate and distinct activity. The problem with relying on qualitative information to identify opportunities is that it constrains thinking.

Threats. When examining threats, the company should focus on two areas: threats to the company's operations and threats to the license to operate. For example, are there any current or emerging issues that can curtail or narrow the company's freedom to operate? Are these a consequence of the company's practices or changing expectations? Frequently, threats are the result of shifting expectations that are societal in scope.

In the late 1990s, for example, opposition toward companies' sourcing practices soared. Media reports of working conditions and wages in countries such as Mexico, Thailand, and Vietnam, along with federal government reaction, led to the development of a task force called the White House Apparel Industry Partnership. The task force, which included such companies as Nike, Reebok, L. L. Bean, and Liz Claiborne, developed a system of monitoring standards to assure consumers that the apparel they buy is not made in sweatshops. Composed of members from business, labor, and human rights groups, the task force came to an agreement in the spring of 1997 on maximum hours (60) and minimum ages of employees (14). It also set wage guidelines that followed U.S. wage standards. In addition, groups and organizations established their own guidelines. Duke University requires that all manufacturers using the Duke logo sign a pledge that they do not use sweatshop labor.

Environmental organizations and animal rights groups are also engaging in actions that are shifting expectations on the manufacturing operations of companies. It is important to gauge the range of reactions to the environmental and experimental practices of the company. Many of these demands and shifts in expectations begin at the community level.

The adequacy of services in a community can also be a threat to a company. An inadequate education system is an obstacle to recruiting an adequately trained workforce. It is also an obstacle to attracting managerial personnel. Managers want to locate in or near communities that provide superior education for their children. It is no accident that the computer industry got its start in Boston and the Silicon Valley. Both communities at that time had the best public and private education systems in the world.

The second area of threat can be toward a company's community contributions programs. The donation of funds to a community organization is viewed as company support for the organization. As was previously indicated, AT&T's contribution to the Planned Parenthood organization created controversy. This is not an isolated incident. American Express was criticized for refusing to contribute to the Boy Scouts in San Francisco because of the agency's policy toward gays. These incidents are likely to expand in response to the growth of single-issue politics.

Opportunities. A company's community programs and actions can also present opportunities. What a company does in the community, as was pointed out, does have ramifications for its reputation and freedom to operate. A company's community involvement provides the opportunity to develop a leadership position in a community, which in turn enables a company to develop support for its operations. An experimental study testing the impact of a company's community programs and responses to community needs and concerns found that individuals would be willing to support a company in a dispute with the government or write letters in support of the company if the firm was actively involved in the community. It was less likely that individuals would support companies that were not involved.[11]

Community involvement also provides an opportunity for a company to shape and improve community services that are necessary to its operations. Companies have been able to redesign public education programs to meet their growing technology needs. IBM and such companies as Eastman Kodak, Bell South, Procter & Gamble, and Boeing are lending their research capabilities to the task of reinventing public education. IBM pledged $10 million to the effort. The intention is to take advantage of a perceived crisis to reshape education to serve the needs of specific businesses.

A few corporations are also using their involvement in the public schools to skim off the "best and the brightest" of high school students as employees. Some, copying the practice of college athletic departments, are offering four-year scholarships to students they identify in their school partnership programs. In return for the scholarships, the students are expected to work for the company once they graduate. Trying to retain a young workforce, business and government in Nebraska have joined together to provide college tuition for students who sign a three-year commitment to stay and work for a company located in Nebraska.

In summary, the strategic category should contain an analysis of the community threats and opportunities facing the company (Figure 7.3).

SOURCES OF INFORMATION

There are five ways to gather the information needed for a community assessment:

Figure 7.3
The Elements of the Factual, Qualitative and Strategic Information for a Community Assessment

Factual	Qualitative	Strategic
Community data	Community attitudes, concerns, and expectations	Threats
Community needs		Opportunities
Other companies' programs	Company's community reputation	
Community resources		

1. Secondary sources (reports, studies, and publications)
2. Informal meetings with community individuals and groups
3. Planned programs such as regularly scheduled meetings with selected individuals in a community
4. Survey of employees
5. Community interviews and surveys

Secondary Sources

Secondary sources are reports published by government and voluntary organizations. City and county planning agencies are a valuable source of information about the demographics in a community and plans that describe the future programs in the community. In some instances, government social services agencies might have data on the needs in the community.

Again, as I noted earlier, the local United Way is another source of factual information on a community. As part of its planning and problem-solving mission, United Ways conduct community needs assessments. Published reports of the studies are readily available to any company and should be part of the information resources of the community relations department.

Informal Meetings and Associations

One way companies obtain information about a community is through informal associations. Managers attend meetings at which they learn about issues and problems in a community. Community relations managers frequently meet informally with colleagues and learn about community needs and concerns that prove valuable for planning. Companies depend on the community relations manager to be the primary source of information about the community.

Planned Community Practice Programs

The value of keeping abreast of issues and concerns in a community has induced a number of companies to formalize programs that take advantage of the information that can be gathered at community meetings and events. Merck, for example, asks its managers to take responsibility for attending the meetings of specific community agencies. Some are asked to attend city council, zoning committee, or city planning meetings. Others are asked to attend meetings of nonprofit organizations. And still others are asked to use their volunteer activity as a way to obtain information on needs and concerns. It has long been customary, for example, for public affairs managers to attend legislative and government agency meetings to keep informed of government issues that could affect a company.

A secondary value of formalizing meetings and associations with community individuals and groups is that it provides opportunities for fostering and maintaining relationships that build trust in a community. In fact, for some companies, this is a key value of community involvement.

Employee Interviews

Although interviewing employees for information on what role the company should play in a community was recommended in Chapter 4, it deserves repeating. Employees are a valued source of community information. They are also valued by the company. For those two reasons alone, employees' opinions should be sought whenever a company is conducting an external analysis.

The Boeing Company, for example, periodically surveys employees for information on a wide range of issues related to community charities and community relations.[12] Conducted for the company by research consultants, the survey seeks information from employees on the way the company conducts solicitations for major charities, such as the United Way. It also asks for opinions on other types of solicitations for charities by employees, such as tickets, chances, and collection boxes. In addition, the company looks to the employees to identify the problems in the community and asks employees for their evaluation of selected charities in the community. The company finds this information not only useful for internal planning but also helpful in identifying issues in the community that can likely impact the company.

Surveys and Interviews of Community Residents

Probably the most reliable source of information on needs, community concerns, and attitudes are the residents in a community. Consequently, a few companies have sample surveyed residents. In 1995, for example, IBM surveyed 1,574 households in five cities—Atlanta, Boston, Detroit, Raleigh-Durham, and San Francisco. IBM was particularly interested in the affect of community relations on consumer purchasing. The findings supported results similar to other such studies. Consumers (76.8 percent) were influenced by a company's community relations activities.[13]

In 1981 the First Bank of Minneapolis conducted a survey on quality-of-life issues and concerns in its city. The findings, which were reported in the *Minneapolis Tribune*, were extensive and covered such areas as education, jobs, public safety, and culture and recreation.[14] Merck is another company that periodically surveys residents in plant cities for information about community issues and attitudes toward the company.

There are companies, too—the Southern California Gas Company is an example—that include in periodic surveys on customer satisfaction questions on their community relations programs. The purpose is to determine the level of awareness of the company's community relations programs and to obtain ideas on community needs.

OPINION LEADER SURVEYS

Conducting large-scale resident surveys is costly. The benefits, moreover, for program planning are questionable. Consequently, many companies have abandoned extensive community resident surveys in favor of seeking the opinions of a limited number of selected individuals—20 to 40 key opinion leaders. In fact, companies that do survey all or a sample of the community residents frequently also seek the opinions of a select group of opinion leaders to enrich their findings.

Key leaders often reflect opinions on community issues and concerns. They also are involved in community programs and events. In many instances, key leaders are the definers of community attitudes and perceptions; so their opinions are valuable.

Key leader interviews, which can be conducted by telephone, in person, or in focus groups, run from 45 minutes to an hour in length. They commonly focus on five general areas:

1. Opinions on the priority ranking of community needs or problems
2. Factual questions related to knowledge of a company's existing programs—example, are they aware of the company's partnership with a local school
3. Comparison of the company's community reputation with other companies in the community
4. Recommendations for the company's focus
5. Opinions on attitudes about the company's reputation

CHOOSING KEY LEADERS FOR INTERVIEWS

The question, of course, is, Who should be involved in a needs assessment survey? As was explained in Chapter 6, there are many different sources of influence or leadership in a community. Some are formal leaders based on their position in the community. Others are informal leaders who are able to influence the formation and resolution of issues because of their involvement in community affairs and organizations. Some companies select key leaders from both categories. They interview, for example, the mayor, the head of the United Way, the president of the hospital board, the newspaper publisher, or a CEO of a major company, for example.

While it is important to seek the opinions of these types of leaders, there are others in a community that can supply information that is equally as valuable in determining community needs, concerns, and issues. Leaders of environmental organizations or the head of a small neighborhood association or settlement house may be able to provide important information that can help in developing a community program that addresses a severe and serious community need. They also may be able to supply information on broader issues of concern that may impact on the future plans and goals of a company.

For this reason, I have found it helpful when working with companies to rely on a categorical scheme that includes four types of key leaders: formal leaders and leaders of three types of influence organizations—mediating, advocacy, and sentiment. *Formal* leaders are people with legitimate authority because of their position in the community; for example, mayors, superintendents of schools, heads of governmental departments, and executive directors of community based organizations.

Mediating organizations are the most common type of community-based organization. Mediating organizations act on behalf of the interests of a particular constituency (local businesspeople, professionals, elderly, children, cancer victims, homeowners, for example); other organizations (social service agencies, service clubs, trade and industrial associations); or the community (community planning and federated fund-raising organizations like the United Way). Their major activities are problem solving, planning, and promoting the programs and interests of the organization. A distinguishing characteristic of mediating organizations is that they seek to achieve their ends by using consensus, education, and persuasion. Rarely do they engage in confrontational tactics.

Confrontation, contention, and demonstrations are the tactics that distinguish another type of influence organization—*advocacy* or activist organizations. Advocacy organizations act on behalf of the needs, interests, and aspirations of a specific constituency. They promote the adoption of a single cause—gun control, education of the handicapped, protection for abused children, needs and services of the elderly, abortion rights, clean air, or a sustainable environment, for example. They promote the needs of the constituency in the larger community and engage in a variety of methods to achieve the constituency's goals. Methods can range from persuasion to confrontation, demonstrations, contention, and even violence.

A third type of influence organization is the *sentiment group*. Identified by sociologist Charles Willie in studies of hospital planning in Syracuse, New York, sentiment groups are organizations meeting the association and information needs of individuals and groups. Frequently, they have a widespread base of formal and informal members and, consequently, are a source of the sentiments and concerns of many people in a community. Sentiment groups, which include religious organizations, ethnic associations, historical societies, library groups, voter education organizations, and trade unions, rarely get involved in promoting or initiating community action. In fact, they have little success in initiating an action or program in a community. Where they are often successful, however, is in vetoing action.[15]

This is not an exclusive typology. Individuals can be members of more than one type of influence group. An opinion leader of a mediating organization can also be associated with a sentiment group. The Catholic bishop, for example, can be a prominent member of the United Way board and also a leader of the Catholic sentiment community. The president of the NAACP, a sentiment organization, can also be the president of the United Way. And some can have formal and informal leadership roles. A member of the city council could also be a prominent board member of a community development corporation. It is useful to identify people that represent more than one influence group—*twofers* or *threefers* is what community planners call such people.

It is also an "ideal" type of categorization; thus, it is not a strict, impermeable categorization. Organizations, for example, can move from one type to another or even share the methods of more than one type of influence organization. In the 1950s the United Way, for example, was a strong and vocal advocate for a single fund-raising campaign for all community charities. They used persuasion and pressure to prevent corporations from contributing to health campaigns such as Cancer, Heart, and Polio.

Then, too, organizations move from one category to another, from activist organization to mediating organization. In fact, research indicates that activists or advocacy groups become less confrontational over time, particularly after they begin to attract a broader base of membership. This forces the organization to use the methods common to mediating organizations: consensus and education. One sociologist called this an iron law of community organizations.[16]

Despite these limitations, the categorical scheme is a helpful guide to the selection of key leaders to be involved in needs assessment surveys and interviews. It is also a useful guide for identifying people for relationship building programs, discussed in the next chapter. The selection, therefore, of individuals to interview for opinions on needs, issues, and concerns in a community should include representatives of four categories, as depicted in Figure 7.4. The number and type of key leaders to select for a needs assessment depend on the scope of the study and the size of the community. Commonly, 20 to 30 key leaders are selected. Some are interviewed in person and others by telephone.

Figure 7.4
Identifying Key Leaders for Sources of Information

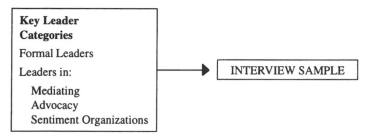

ISSUES TO CONSIDER IN CONDUCTING A NEEDS AND ISSUES ASSESSMENT

Scope

The first issue that needs to be considered before conducting a needs assessment is scope. How extensive should it be? This very much depends on the information needed to make decisions. A complete redesign of the community relations activities and programs will require a comprehensive assessment including information from secondary sources as well as information on attitudes, issues, needs, and opinions from a sample of community residents. It should also include information from employees and key leaders. This will not only provide information to make decisions on program design but also will provide a baseline of information for evaluation and further planning. On the other hand, if the information is needed to refocus a contributions program, then the opinions of key leaders and employees may be all that are necessary.

Scope also depends on the type of industry. Some industries, particularly oil, chemical, and pharmaceutical companies, are constantly faced with the need to reassure communities that their manufacturing operations are harmless and have a low-risk factor. Indeed, government regulations require reporting of chemical hazards and communicating to communities scenarios on what could happen if a chemical accident occurred.[17]

When, for example, Van G. Long, now vice president for Health, Safety and Environmental Affairs for Rhone-Poulenc, was appointed to head up one of the company's pharmaceutical plants in Kanawha Valley, West Virginia, he requested a detailed report on the community, including its culture, its traditions, its values, its way of life, how decisions were made, the identity of key people, and the quality of existing relationships, along with quantitative data on demographics and community service programs. Prepared by a consultant, the report was almost 500 pages in length. It proved invaluable as a complete orientation to the new community. It served as a very helpful guide to Long when he had to plan a community report and forum on the worst risk that the community would face if an accidental hazardous incident occurred. It enabled him to identify the people to be involved in planning the forum. The forum, in turn, proved to be a guide to developing trust relationships with key individuals in the community.[18]

Frequency

A comprehensive and formal needs assessment should only be conducted every three to five years. Because of its relationship building value, however, procedures should be put in place to obtain information from key leaders on a regular basis. Techniques for doing this will be explained more fully in the next chapter.

SUMMARY

The community assessment is the second step in the information- or data-gathering process for designing strategies to implement the neighbor of choice principle. Three categories of information are needed—factual, qualitative, and strategic.

Figure 7.5 is a summary and planning guide for identifying the information that may need to be collected in a community assessment. The vertical axis lists all the types of communities to which a company may have to respond. (See Chapter 5 for a description of the communities.) The horizontal axis lists the information that should be obtained from each type of community.

NOTES

1. W. A. Kimmel, "Needs Assessment: A Critical Perspective," in *Readings in Community Organization Practice*, 3rd ed., ed. H. Specht and R. M. Kramer (Englewood Cliffs, NJ: Prentice-Hall, 1969).

2. United Way of America, *Focus on Program Outcomes: Survey Guide* (Alexandria, VA: United Way of America, 1996).

3. Mitsubishi Electric America Foundation, *Road Map: Creating and Sustaining Project Impact: Guidelines for Evaluation and Dissemination* (Washington, D.C.: Mitsubishi Electric Foundation, n.d.).

4. Council on Foundations, *Corporate Update Newsletter*, Winter 1997, p. 5.

5. K. B. Murray and V. M. Vogel, "Using a Hierarchy-of-Effects Approach to Gauge the Effectiveness of Corporate Social Responsibility to Generate Goodwill toward the Firm: Financial versus Nonfinancial Impacts," *Journal of Business Research*, Vol. 38 (1997), p. 143.

6. S. Z. Ryan, "Fleet Financial Commits $8.5 Billion to Minorities, Low-Income Borrowers," *Wall Street Journal*, February 9, 1994.

7. R. Barnes and N. Goldberg, "Glaxo Senior Management Survey," Community Needs Assessment (Chestnut Hill, MA: Center for Corporate Community Relations at Boston College, May 1994).

Figure 7.5
Community Assessment Framework

COMMUNITY ANALYSIS	Leaders	Current Relationships	Needs	Attitudes	Expectations	Reputation	Concerns
Site							
Employee							
Fenceline							
Impact							
operations							
influence							
entry							
exit							
Cyber							
Functional							
ethnic							
environment							
education							
religious							
children							
etc.							

8. C. J. Fombrun, *Reputation: Realizing Value from the Corporate Image* (Boston: Harvard Business School Press, 1996).

9. Levi Strauss & Co., "Global Corporate Reputation," notes on presentation, n.d., San Francisco, CA.

10. Ibid.

11. Murray and Vogel, "Using a Hierarchy-of-Effects Approach," pp. 152–155.

12. W. S. Brown, *1996 Boeing Community Relations Study: Methodological Overview and Weighted Data Tables with Questionnaire* (Edmonds, WA: First Northwest Group, 1996).

13. R. Barnes, *Measurement of Consumer Reaction to Socially Responsible Companies: A Research Report from The Center for Corporate Community Relations at Boston College* (Chestnut Hill, MA: The Center for Corporate Community Relations at Boston College, 1994).

14. K. Troy, *Studying and Addressing Community Needs: A Corporate Case Book* (New York: Conference Board, 1985).

15. C. V. Willie, "A Success Story of Community Action," *Nursing Outlook*, Vol. 9, no. 1 (January 1961), pp. 19–20.

16. Columbia University Bureau of Applied Social Research, *The Volunteers: Means and Ends in a National Organization*, a report by David L. Sill (Glencoe, IL: Free Press, 1957).

17. All manufacturing companies, incidentally, are required by the Federal Emergency Planning and Community Right-to-Know Act to inform state and community emergency planners and community fire departments about hazardous chemicals on plant sites. For chemical companies that deal with a great many hazardous materials, this requirement presents formidable problems. Detailed information on a community may be critical for such companies.

18. V. Long, "Worst Case Scenario Process: Kanawha Valley, WV" (presentation at RMP/Regulatory Issues Seminar, Chemical Industry Council of NJ, New Brunswick, NJ, November 18, 1997); interview with author, November 18, 1997.

Part III

The Three Strategies

Chapter 8

The First Strategy:
Building Relationships of Trust

for "neighbor of choice"

The purpose of the company and community assessments is to provide information for program planning. They are complementary activities that form the knowledge base of the company's plan for becoming a neighbor of choice. Figure 8.1 depicts the relationship of the internal and external assessments to the next steps for implementing the neighbor of choice principle.

There are three program strategies for implementing the neighbor of choice principle. One is to build trust relationships in communities; another is to identify and monitor issues and concerns that can have a likely impact on the company; and the third is to design community support programs so that they respond to company and community needs.

The focus of this chapter is to describe ways to build sustainable and ongoing relationships in local communities.

BUILDING SUSTAINABLE RELATIONSHIPS

The goal of the neighbor of choice principle, as I explained in Chapter 1, is to build a legacy of trust between a company and its communities. Merck uses the term "community trust account," which is a graphic metaphor to describe the type of trust it wants managers to achieve in their site communities. Based on Stephen Covey's concept of the importance of trust in relationships, Merck explains that the community trust account is the central underpinning of its community strategies. The goal of its strategy is to build up reserves of trust through relationships with key organizations and people and by being honest, responsive, and ethical in the operations of its facilities. This adds value to the trust account, and the company can make occasional withdrawals and use the account for leverage or collateral—as long as the trust account remains positive.[1]

Figure 8.1
Elements of the Company and Community Assessments and the Neighbor of Choice Strategies

Source: Adapted from A. C. Hax and N. S. Majulf, *The Strategy Concept and Process: A Pragmatic Approach*, 2nd ed. (Upper Saddle River, NJ: Prentice-Hall, 1996), p. 29.

The principal way to build trust is through relationships—sustainable relationships with key individuals and organizations in the community. Relationships of trust, however, are not achieved easily, casually, or quickly. They are not developed by just getting to know people or attending community functions. They depend, first, upon the company's record of integrity in the community. Is the company honest, fair, and consistent in its operations and its relationships with individuals in the community?

Equally important, developing relationships of trust requires competency. They cannot be left to chance. It is a management function requiring technical and conceptual skills. The goal is not to develop friendships—although this could be an accidental consequence—but to forge relationships that use transactions that add value to the community trust account. There are two objectives to the relationship—a process objective and a procedural objective.

The process objective includes the skills of listening, communicating, and creating win-win situations. It demands a sense of empathy, the ability to understand but not necessarily agree with the feelings and concerns of others.[2] This is a skill that managers often find difficult to acquire because they have been ill prepared in their education or by experience to learn it.

There are two procedural objectives. One involves planning and implementing programs that facilitate and enhance relationships. The second is managing expectations or managing what I have called the psychological contract described in Chapter 1. There are four ways to manage the psychological contract.

MANAGING THE PSYCHOLOGICAL CONTRACT

Recognize the Contract Exists

The contract must be recognized. Managers have to understand that it is not a social contract. It is a concept that describes not just the common expectations that one person would have for another but also expectations of shared ideals. Some of these are quite explicit. People in communities, including companies, are engaged jointly in building and supporting institutions that define a "good" community, the ego ideal of a community, as a psychologist would define it. These include schools, roads, parks, recreation facilities, fire protection, police, cultural institutions, human services to protect the frail and needy, hospitals, and the like. Implicitly, there is an expectation that everyone pays their fair share to support these institutions. And people, as I said earlier, want to live in communities that are clean, environmentally safe, friendly, and cooperative.

Establish a Procedure and Plans for Identifying the Implicit Expectations

Developing trust relationships for managing the psychological contract cannot be done without a program and a plan. There are a number of different programs that companies are using to establish sustainable relationships in communities. These are described below.

One of the aims of any relationship building program is to get people (key leaders) to discuss their expectations for the company. This does not imply that the company will respond to the expectations. But it does mean that the company will acknowledge the expectation and be willing to negotiate it.

Many companies are fearful of exploring expectations with community leaders. They feel they may be opening up a can of worms or, worse, creating unrealistic expectations. But this need not be the case. People are generally willing to negotiate issues and concerns, provided that a trust relationship exists. In fact, companies such as Disney, Monsanto, and Wal-Mart were rebuffed in their decisions to move into communities precisely because they violated the contract. They were unwilling or unable to discuss the communities' expectations and consequently were left with no negotiating position.

Define the Realities

Companies need not be put in a position that they are constantly reacting to expectations. A company has to define the realities: What it can do and cannot do; what is negotiable and what is not.

The company need not accept all criticism or angry behavior from the community. Unacceptable behavior has to be contained. People in a community have to be held accountable for behaving and operating effectively. A company does not have to excuse behavior that is unwarranted. It does, however, have to manage it. When there are expressions of anger or behaviors that reflect anger, it is important to try and understand what the behavior means. Newspaper articles, for example, critical of a company's operational performance need to be explored disinterestedly. Only after that process can a company make a realistic and workable decision. Operational decisions, in other words, should not be made by drift or by chance.

Continually Reinforce the Necessity of Managing the Psychological Contract

Companies like Merck recognize that they cannot expect their managers to achieve competency in developing trust relationships without training. If they are not trained or sensitive to the requirements of developing trust relationships, they are likely to destroy credibility for the company. When Kraft was attempting to build a football stadium in South Boston (described in Chapter 6), he assumed that the residents would bow to the demands of the political leaders. Kraft was perceived as an outsider who did not consult with the residents. He further alienated the residents when he claimed he spent "nearly a $1 million on Irish consultants."[3] It was inevitable that the plan would fail.

Not only does management have to acknowledge the existence of the psychological contract, but it has to be continually reinforced through training. It is not unlikely that companies with exemplary community reputations violate the psychological contract. Managers, on occasion, act in haste, or they may be unmindful of expectations that have shifted.

The Polaroid Corporation, for example, needlessly stirred up community anger in two communities when it began exploring sites for moving its headquarters. Polaroid, it should be pointed out, has an enviable community reputation in Massachusetts, based on the values and philosophy of founder Edwin Land, which the company has continued to maintain. The company is praised both in the press and by advocacy groups for its commitment to communities, despite the fact that it is one of the largest polluters in the state. Polaroid began thinking of moving its headquarters from Cambridge to Waltham, a western suburb, in 1995. The company pledged to the mayor of Cambridge that he would be informed before a final decision was made. Without notifying anyone in the company or the community, the company's real estate manager formally applied to the Waltham City Council for a height variance on its plans to build the headquarters. The neighbors showed up at the zoning committee hearing to protest. The next day a front-page article describing the meeting appeared in the *Waltham News Tribune*. The *Tribune* also criticized Polaroid. The city manager of Cambridge was outraged.

The company quickly began meeting with the neighbors, explaining its actions. The company's previous trust relationships helped it to allay the neighbors' fears, and the variance was approved at a subsequent hearing. Polaroid had to apologize personally to the Cambridge city manager.

Merck has a similar example. In West Point, Pennsylvania, Merck bought a parcel of undeveloped farmland in 1991 when it was expanding a plant. Gradually the land adjacent to the site Merck purchased was developed into housing units. As operations at the plant expanded, Merck was pressed for additional space. The company began using trailers as temporary offices to house staff.

A decision was made in 1996 to use more of the original unused parcel of land to build an office. One resident protested Merck's plans and was able to galvanize others to protest. The residents surrounding the facility rose in opposition. At the first zoning board hearing, after three months of work, the board would not give Merck permission to build on its land.

The expectations of the community for the land had changed since Merck originally bought it. The residents purchased land and built homes in what they assumed was a residential area. The company, on the other hand, assumed that their original expectation and the literal contract with the community still held. The psychological contract, in other words, had been violated.

Over another three months, Merck staff began meeting with the resident group to make its case. The company's previous work in the community, its legacy of trust as a consequence of good relationships, and its skill in renegotiating the expectations led to a different but acceptable decision. The zoning board approved the redesigned Merck plan. In April of 1998 the leader of the opposition to Merck's expansion plans was present at the spade-turning ceremony.

RELATIONSHIP BUILDING OUTREACH PROGRAMS

The aim of the relationship building strategy is to develop what I have termed community practice programs that open up dialogue and discussion with key individuals and groups in all the defined communities in which the firm does business. Companies are using a variety of community practice programs to build and sustain positive relationships in a community.

Plant Tours and Programs

One of the most popular community practice programs is to invite residents to tour a plant or view the company in operation. Viewed initially as an unwanted disruption of the workplace, plant tours have become fairly common. Even the military, long accustomed to using secrecy to avoid inconvenience, provides tours of installations and warships.

A variation on the plant tour is to invite residents to attend a festival or program on the company site. Sometimes a simple fair for children can bring surprising results. In Oiso, Japan, in the early 1990s a chemical plant wanted to build a facility on the outskirts of the community. A local teacher, concerned about the environmental affects of the company, began a campaign in the community to oppose the company. His efforts were successful. The plant was not given the permits to locate in Oiso. Subsequently, the teacher was elected mayor of the town. The plant manager of the S. C. Johnson Wax Company located in Oiso was concerned that the new mayor would be antagonistic to his company. "Oh, no," the mayor told the Johnson Wax manager. "You are a good company, well respected and well liked in our community." One reason the company enjoyed the respect of the community, according to the mayor, was an annual ice cream festival held by Johnson Wax for the schoolchildren and their families on the plant's grounds.

Encouraging the Use of Facilities by Nonprofits

Another popular technique is to allow nonprofit organizations to use the meeting room facilities. In some instances, companies have allowed groups of nonprofits to set up volunteer organizing booths in the company lobbies. Procter & Gamble held a community organization fair in its lobby to show support for the United Way.

Companies have also opened up their training programs for nonprofit executives. This serves two purposes. It provides much needed training in management for nonprofit executives, and it also helps to promote positive relationships—in other words, building up credits in the trust account.

Engaging Key Leaders in Planning Activities

An innovative method companies have used to build trust relationships is by involving key leaders in the community assessment process. By seeking the suggestions of key leaders in a community for advice on how the company should set priorities for its contributions programs develops support and respect. In fact, the mere asking for advice on the focus of contributions programs enhances the community reputation of a company. Companies have found it to be the simplest and most inexpensive method for demonstrating the company's sincere interest in improving a community's quality of life.

When COMSAT, the satellite company, for example, was in the process of deciding on the focus of its contribution programs, it interviewed a number of government and community leaders for their advice on the major issues in the District of Columbia and for their opinions on what issues the company should focus for their contributions. This action both surprised and impressed those who were interviewed. Representative Edward Markey, then chairman of the Subcommittee on Telecommunications and Finance of the U.S. House of Representatives' Commerce Committee, which had oversight responsibility for COMSAT, praised the company for its action even though his suggested issue, crime and delinquency, was not selected by the company. The company chose education as its focus issue.

Another example: Dayton Hudson has appointed key customers to its charitable contributions committee as a way to obtain community information and at the same time build relationships with customers.

Key Contact Programs

A community practice program used by many companies in a variety of ways is the "key contact program." Using a community leader identification method similar to the one described in Chapter 7, individuals are identified in any of the communities that have an influence in preserving the company's license to operate. Examples would include the head of a homeowners' association, mayor, hospital president, newspaper publisher, and president of the United Way—representatives of the formal leadership and leaders in mediating, advocacy, and sentiment organizations.

Periodically, but on a regularly scheduled basis, once or twice a year, the key contacts are asked for their views on a variety of facts—current community issues, image of the company, and indications of shifting expectations toward the firm and business in general are some examples. An objective of the key contact meeting is to get these people to talk about their expectations.

Merck has a key contact program that it has found beneficial in developing and maintaining trust relationships. A variety of managers (human resources, environmental engineer, operations departments, for example) are assigned a community leader.

The opinions of the key contact should be sought regarding any changes the company is contemplating, particularly changes that could have an impact—positively or negatively—on the community.

A variation of the key contact is the *organizational contact program*. The goal of the organizational contact program is to ensure that the firm is represented by managers as volunteers in community organizations. These might include educational task forces, chambers of commerce, industrial or trade associations, United Ways, service clubs, environmental organizations, recreational associations, children's agencies, and settlement houses.

There are a number of purposes to the organizational contact program. One is to provide support and expertise to community agencies and organizations, particularly those organizations that are receiving financial contributions from the firm. A second is to ensure that the company is widely represented in the community. This requires that the firm establish a strategically planned volunteer placement program. Managers are assisted and encouraged to participate in organizations selected by the firm. A third is to use participation in organizations to become aware of attitudes and issues that have a potential impact on the firm. And the fourth is to build trust through relationships developed in the volunteer activities.

Community Advisory Panels

Growing in popularity, particularly among companies that have very sensitive operational relationships in communities, such as chemical and oil companies, are community advisory panels (CAPs). The Chemical Manufacturers Association, an association of chemical companies, has been a leading proponent of CAPs. The Association provides technical assistance to companies in the formation and operation of such panels.[4] In 1991 there were 56 CAPs within the chemical industry. By 1996 this number had grown to 316.

Community advisory panels serve as a liaison between a company or any of its facilities and its community. They provide a structure for addressing community concerns and questions about a company. Community advisory panels, according to David Strong, manager of Neighborhood Relationships for Eastman Kodak Company, are important because they tend to focus on the quality-of-life issues in a neighborhood or community—noise, odors, and the appearance of a facility, for example.[5] More important, it is a constructive relationship building technique that has proven successful for managing the expectations of local groups.

There are four kinds of CAPs. One is an *ad hoc panel* convened periodically to advise the company or a facility. They are convened by a facility manager customarily for a specific project. Or in some instances they are used to test the feasibility of a formal CAP.

The *company* or *facility organized* CAP is a second type. This is a formalized CAP organized and supported by the company or facility. The panel generally elects its own chairperson, and the company provides staff support and structure for the panel.

A third type is a *consortium* of a number of companies or facilities within an industry. They function as a company panel providing information about the needs and concerns in a community but allowing the companies or facilities to solve problems and pursue mutual goals.

Independently organized panels set up by a third party constitute the fourth type. The League of Women Voters, for example, has been contracted to set up and staff panels for companies or facilities. These types tend to provide more open communication and a truer sense of the community concerns and needs than panels organized by companies.

While the purpose of CAPs is to serve as a liaison between the company and the community, they have also served other goals for both companies and communities. Some companies rely on CAPs to help focus their contribution programs. The manager of the Chemical Division of Reilly Industries in Indianapolis, Indiana, reports, "The establishment of community advisory panels really caused us to rethink our corporate contributions programs. One result is that monetary and time contributions are being more tightly focused on the community in the immediate vicinity of the plant."[6]

For some companies, particularly those in rural areas, the community advisory panel serves as a community agency serving the development and leadership needs of the community. LASMO Oil in Colombia set up community action committees in urban areas and hamlets in the Casanare and Espinal Districts where the company had drilling and refining operations. The committees helped to improve the educational, social, and health needs of their communities despite the disruption caused by guerrillas in some of the communities. The company was able to increase its trust and overcome the conflictual problems that once hindered the company's freedom to operate.[7]

Olin Corporation has a highly developed community advisory panels program in fifteen communities. It provides training, supports national meetings of its community CAPS, and provides facilitators to run the meetings. The overall goal of the CAPs, reports Laura Tew, director of Community Outreach for the Olin Corporation, is to help the company "become a Neighbor of Choice."[8]

A company cannot assume that a community advisory panel will deter the formation of a neighborhood group critical of the company's actions. Bristol-Myers Squibb had formed a community advisory panel to work with its fermentation plant in Syracuse, New York. In response to a tax issue, another group, the Committee to Preserve Eastwood Heights, emerged expressing concerns about the emissions and operations of the plant. The group complained about noise coming from the plant, a blinking strobe light atop a plant stack, and odors and health risks associated with living near the plant. The group believed they were entitled to a tax abatement for living so close to the plant.

Bristol-Myers Squibb's relationships in the community, developed by its community relations manager Charles Borgognoni, enabled it to overcome any potential public criticism. The company indicated it could not comment on tax issues but was willing to work with the group over its concerns with the operations of the plant. At its first meeting Bristol-Myers Squibb invited the Eastwood Heights Committee to choose someone to serve on the company's community advisory panel. This went a long way in allaying the community's fears and criticism. The minutes of the meeting stated, "Bristol is very open to continue to discuss and assist our neighborhood group. We are very pleased with the process and look forward to a working relationship with our corporate neighbor.'' A study conducted by public administration students at Syracuse University also praised the actions of the company.[9]

SUMMARY

A core strategy for becoming a neighbor of choice in communities is through the establishment of relationships—trust relationships. Trust relationships are necessary for two reasons. First, it is a way to build a legacy of trust and therefore maintain and enhance the company's license to operate. Second, it is the means by which a company can renegotiate the expectations a community has for it.

Managing relationships cannot be left to chance. They must be part of a plan for active community involvement. A number of different relationship building plans have been described in this chapter.

NOTES

1. Merck & Co., *A Guide to Becoming a Neighbor of Choice* (Whitehouse Station, NJ: Merck & Co., 1997), p. 9.

2. S. R. Covey, *First Things First to Live, to Love, to Learn, to Leave a Legacy* (New York: Simon & Schuster, 1994), pp. 240–241.

3. C. M. Sennott and T. Cassidy, "How Kraft's Grand Plan Unraveled," *Boston Globe*, February 23, 1997, p. 24.

4. The Chemical Manufacturers Association publishes material on CAPs, and it is a source of the description of community advisory panels in this book. See Chemical Manufacturers Association, *Advisory Panels: Options for Community Outreach* (Washington, D.C.: Chemical Manufacturers Association, n.d.).

5. David Strong, Interview with author, Santa Barbara, CA, March 17, 1998.

6. A. Naude, "Let's Get Local. Chemical Companies Community Outreach Programs," *Chemical Marketing Reporter*, October 13, 1994.

7. LASMO Oil (Colombia) Limited, "Activities Indicators and Assessment of Impact of Community Relations Programme," Research and Evaluation Report, Santa Fe de Bogotá, LASMO Oil (Colombia) Limited, July 1997.

8. L. Tew, "Community Outreach," training material used by company dated September 18, 1996.

9. Center for Corporate Community Relations at Boston College, "Paper Examines Good Relationship between Community Group and Bristol-Myers Squibb—and How It Got That Way," *Community Relations Letter*, Vol. 12, no. 2 (October 1997), p. 3.

Chapter 9

The Second Strategy: Managing Community Issues and Concerns

In the spring of 1974, Nancy Wertheimer, a psychologist in Colorado, began studying the possible link between leukemia and infections among children in Denver. She found no association or unusual clusters, but what she did find was a strange connection between the incidence of childhood leukemia and the location of electrical transformers near the homes of children stricken with the disease. While there was only a faint correlation, she found that the disease was higher among children living in close proximity to the transformers. She also discovered that it dropped off sharply the further the children's homes were from transformers.[1]

In collaboration with a physicist friend, Ed Leeper, she began investigating the phenomenon by measuring the strength of electromagnetic fields (EMFs) with a scientific instrument called a gauss meter. This led her to discover that the leukemia clusters were not related to transformers but to the high-energy wires emanating from the transformers. She expanded her investigation to other areas in greater Denver. She continued studying the relationship between the leukemia clusters and high-energy wires through 1976, 1977, and part of 1978. Her study was unfunded; consequently, her investigation was all conducted on her own time.

In collaboration with her physicist friend, an article on her findings was accepted by the *American Journal of Epidemiology*, a widely respected peer review journal published by the Johns Hopkins School of Hygiene and Public Health. It appeared in the March 1979 issue and was entitled "Electrical Wiring Configurations and Childhood Cancer."[2] Wertheimer and Leeper concluded that "the homes of children who developed cancer were found unduly often near electrical lines carrying high current."[3]

At first her article attracted limited attention. One industry analyst commented that her analysis did not include examining the strength of EMFs within the homes of the children. Except for one or two, most scientists ignored her findings.

In 1979 an article appeared in *The Saturday Review* highly critical of a National Academy of Sciences' committee investigating the effect of EMFs on children. Entitled "The Invisible Threat: The Stifled Story of Electric Waves," it heated up the controversy and set scientist against scientist.[4] The chair of the National Academy of Sciences committee threatened to sue *The Saturday Review* unless there was a retraction. The magazine refused.

The electric industry began refuting Wertheimer's claims and attacking her research. Studies they had conducted found no relationship. Nonetheless, Wertheimer insisted that a majority of scientific studies conducted in the 1980s supported her findings that there was an association between exposure to electromagnetic fields and the development of cancer. She also cited findings from studies conducted in Sweden. A 1992 article in the *New England Journal of Medicine* reporting that the occupational exposure to EMFs could be a cause for cancer was also used to support her arguments.

The bulk of the debate during this time was carried out among epidemiologists and in scientific journals. The debate heated up when news of incidents of cancer among children living or going to school near high-tension wires was subsequently reported in other communities. A doctor in Montecito, California, a small community near Santa Barbara, for example, reported to officials of the county health department what he thought was a high incidence of leukemia and lymphoma among children in his community. An investigation by the state department of health services revealed that almost five times the expected number of leukemia and lymphoma diagnoses among children in a population the size of Montecito's occurred between 1981 and 1988. The only common element discovered after exhaustive research was that the children all went to the same school—the Montecito Union School. Crossing the school's property was a high-tension wire coming from an electrical substation adjacent to the school's kindergarten playground.

In Guilford, Connecticut a cluster of cancer incidents was reported on Meadow Street, which was also the location of an electrical substation. Similar reports of cancer clusters near electrical substations and high-tension wires were also reported in San Diego, China Grove and Dukeville, North Carolina.

In each instance, the discovery of the clusters was made by a local resident. In Guilford a design and product development consultant learned of the strange clusters of cancer on Meadow Street from a friend whose daughter, a girlfriend of the consultant's son, became ill with cancer. The daughter's parents believed the cause of the cancer and the cancers of a dozen other residents of Meadow Street was the electrical substation. On his own the consultant began reading about the relationship between EMFs and cancer. He initiated inquiries from the local Connecticut power company.

In North Carolina it was a doctor who became interested in the issue as a consequence of the numbers of brain tumors reported to him. Brain cancer was a rare occurrence in Tampa, where he had practiced for over 20 years. When he moved to Salisbury, North Carolina, in October 1988, he was struck by the unusually high number of cases of brain cancer. Four cases were referred to him in one week. Subsequent research revealed similar clusters of brain cancer in the county. The one common element: They all lived near high-tension wires. Subsequent studies by the doctor in other North Carolina communities revealed similar occurrences.

In each instance, too, the incidents received their first exposure to the public from local newspapers. The *New Haven Register*, Salisbury (North Carolina) *Post*, and *Montecito Life*, a weekly, for example, each published news accounts of the cancer among children and the possible connection between the cancer and the high-tension wires and substations. The Salisbury *Post* published a series of articles on the issue in 1989. The *New York Times* gave coverage to the story in July 1989.

Power companies at first ignored the emerging studies reporting on the relationship between EMFs and childhood cancer. They often refused to talk to residents or neighborhood groups about the issue. In many instances, as the controversy began heating up, they began personally attacking residents who complained, calling some "trouble makers who don't even live in the neighborhood." Researchers were denounced, and some even lost funding as a consequence of power company pressures. *Montecito Life* was criticized for reporting on the incidents, and it was blamed for bringing down property values in the community.[5]

The issue received its first national exposure in an article by professional writer John Brodeur in the June and July 1990 issues of *The New Yorker*.[6] Brodeur had previously written about the relationships between radar and cancer and asbestos and cancer. His articles were expanded and published in books. The first was titled *Currents of Death: Power Lines, Computer Terminals, and the Attempt to Cover Up the Threat to Your Health*. The second, published in 1993, was called *The Great Power Line Cover-Up: How the Government and the Utilities Are Trying to Hide the Cancer Hazards by Electromagnetic Fields*.[7]

As a consequence of the national attention to the issue, the power companies and industry trade associations began printing brochures and pamphlets assuring communities that there was a spurious connection between EMFs and cancer. They accused the media of relying on unsubstantiated data. They hired their own epidemiologists to conduct studies, who reported that people were more likely to get exposed to high levels of EMFs from toasters or coffeemakers than they were from living directly under high-tension wires. This did not still the debate or the controversy.

For close to ten years, charges and countercharges were hurled back and forth between the industry and its researchers and other researchers supporting the relationship between EMFs and childhood cancer. As the issue was given wider and wider publicity, organizations began to appear to confront power companies

and its national industry spokespersons. In Seattle, for example, Citizens against
Overhead Power Lines successfully prevented Seattle City Light, a municipally
owned power company, from constructing overhead power lines. Organizations
began lobbying for legislation that would require moving high-tension wires
near residential areas and schools. Newsletters supporting the relationship between EMFs and childhood leukemia were started, giving the controversy even
wider publicity. A cottage industry of tort lawyers, engineers who measure energy fields, and writers grew and expanded.

While the debate raged on, government studies began to emerge, refuting the
notion that leukemia was caused by high-tension wires. A study conducted in
1992 by the White House Office of Science and Technology Policy found no
evidence linking power lines with leukemia. A National Academy of Sciences
study in 1996 arrived at similar conclusions.

The critics were not stilled. Parents were urged to move children's beds away
from wall sockets. Housing prices near power lines fell. Power companies were
sued. *Consumer Reports* urged caution in using electric blankets. The Office of
Science and Technology estimated that by 1995 the controversy caused the
public between $1 and $3 billion per year in litigation, lost property values,
higher utility bills, and relocated power lines. Dr. Robert Park, a physicist at
the University of Maryland, said that dozens of people have spent their entire
lives on this one problem.[8]

Then in 1997 an elaborate and elegant study, conducted by the National Cancer Institute and childhood leukemia specialists from around the country, was
reported in the *New England Journal of Medicine*. Its conclusion: There is de-
finitively no relationship between leukemia and exposure to EMFs. The study,
according to its authors, was not ambiguous. There were no dangers, they repeated a number of times, from magnetic fields induced by power lines.[9]

Despite this overwhelming evidence, the controversy has not ended. An ep-
idemiologist at the University of North Carolina, Dr. David Savitz, who conducted a small study of childhood leukemia in 1989, commented on the study
by saying, "this is not compelling evidence." "Further research is needed," he
added. Louis Slesin, editor of *Microwave News*, a newsletter that has warned of
the dangers of power lines, is not at all convinced. "I think it's still a wide
open question. We shouldn't close the book yet."[10]

The EMF controversy is a classic example of the characteristics of social
issues, which can best be defined as a controversial subject on which various
individuals and groups have different and sometimes heated points of view. The
issue can be as widely publicized as the EMF controversy or as little noticed as
the concerns of a neighborhood group about the noise, odors, or traffic nuisances
a company makes.

It matters little, moreover, whether an issue is relevant or factual. It is related
to a perception of the issue. David Grier, formerly with the Royal Bank of
Canada, describes an issue as a gap between corporate action and stakeholder
expectations.[11] The manner in which a company responds to the perception

affects its trust quotient in the community. Consequently, to build trust a company needs to learn ways to anticipate and respond to community concerns and issues.

CHARACTERISTICS OF SOCIAL ISSUES

Meaning of Issues

Social issues should be viewed as a reflection of basic concerns people have about themselves and their communities. Environmental issues, for example, express the concerns and fears people have about health and safety. People want to live in communities that are as free as possible of environmental risks, even if their fears or concerns are unfounded. In some cases, they can be concerns that are frightening. People are terrified of radiation, to use the EMF issue as an example. It taps into, as Dr. Charles Stevens, a neurobiologist at the Salk Institute in San Diego, said, ''our primal fears.''[12] Consequently, once concerns become issues, there is a demand for resolution.

Relying on research findings to respond to concerns of this nature is an exercise in frustration. Statistics and studies cannot be used to counter perceptions and emotions. People often respond to concerns and fears by using intuition and emotion.[13] No amount of logic or rational discussion is able to overcome underlying fears. Consequently, what appears to be irrational or illogical to an outsider is perfectly logical and understandable to those involved in the resolution of an issue.

Community Origin of Issues

A second characteristic of issues, particularly today, is that they emerge primarily at the community and even neighborhood levels. The EMF case is a perfect example. In each of the instances, the controversy first appeared in a neighborhood. But there are dozen of other examples. A number of cities, including Boston, Baltimore, New Haven, Los Angeles, and New York, require companies to pay employees more than the national minimum wage. San Francisco requires companies to offer benefits to domestic partners. Four counties in northern California ban localities from purchasing goods or services from companies with ties to Burma. Proposals to ban the sale of handguns are now being fought at the community and state levels. The mayor of North Olmstead, Ohio, is pushing a resolution adopted by his city that bans cities from buying goods or services made with child labor.

Even national issues are played out in the local community. Patrick Buchanan running in the 1995 presidential primary made corporate welfare, long associated with fringe liberal groups, a national issue. He successfully defeated President George Bush in the New Hampshire primary mainly on the issue that tax advantages and financial incentives for corporations were no different than wel-

Figure 9.1
Life Cycle of an Issue

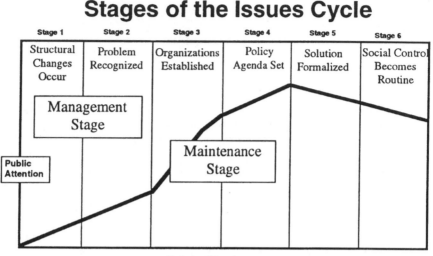

Stages of the Issues Cycle

Stage 1	Stage 2	Stage 3	Stage 4	Stage 5	Stage 6
Structural Changes Occur	Problem Recognized	Organizations Established	Policy Agenda Set	Solution Formalized	Social Control Becomes Routine

Management Stage

Maintenance Stage

Public Attention

Pattern of Development

Source: Used with the permission of Ian Wilson.

fare benefits given to able-bodied men and women. Subsequently, John R. Kasich, Republican from Ohio and chairman of the U.S. House Budget Committee, began championing the issue. He claimed that he could not in good conscience lead the efforts as chairman of the Budget Committee to reduce welfare benefits without insisting that benefits for corporations be excised.

The issue began to be pressed in local communities. Community groups and local newspapers began inquiring about the financial benefits given to companies. Lockheed Martin, for example, was asked by a *Sunnyvale* (CA) *Sun* reporter, "Do you know that the tax advantage you are receiving will hurt the support of our local schools?" A front-page news article published by the paper was critical of the company.[14] When the claim was investigated by Jeannie Dusenberg, the community relations manager of Lockheed Martin, it was discovered that the company had made no such request. One of their vendors did, however. Because the vendor did considerable work for the company, it was assumed that Lockheed Martin was responsible for the request. It was viewed by the community and the newspaper as a Lockheed Martin issue. Prompt response by the community relations manager enabled the issue to be cleared up.[15]

Life Cycle of Issues

Issues tend to go through a predictable pattern of development or life cycle, as it is sometimes called, related to the degree of public attention given to the issue (see Figure 9.1).

At the outset of the development, a structural or technological change occurs. The results of scientific studies can improve technology—for example, DDT's development was a boon to agricultural production. A shift in attitudes, the growth in the numbers of the elderly, and the citizen participation mandates of federal urban renewal and antipoverty legislation are other examples. Little attention is paid to these shifts as they initially occur.

During the second stage, problems become recognized. DDT, for example, would not break down in the soil and was killing fish in streams. A mother claimed that drunk drivers who kill children should be held liable and not excused as participants in an accident of fate. Manufacturers made products that were unsafe and could result in injuries and even death.

The problems, however, do not get noticed or reported by the mainstream newspapers or magazines. They appear first in scientific journals and soon find their way into little-known and small circulation newsletters and magazines. Ralph Nader's description of the dangers of the Corvair automobile, for example, which led to legislation on product safety, first appeared in *Nation Magazine*. Rachel Carson's report on the effects of insecticides on rivers and streams came out in *The New Yorker* before it came out as a book called *Silent Spring*.

It is claimed that during these two emergent stages in the life cycle of an issue an organization can intervene and alter its development. An often cited example is the success companies such as McDonald's and Burger King had in changing the connotation of their industry from servers of "junk food," a phrase common among teenagers in the early 1960s, to servers of "fast food."

As a consequence of these reports and articles, the issue becomes further noticed by the public. Organizations come into existence promoting and advocating for solutions. Shortly after Rachel Carson wrote her book, Greenpeace and the Natural Resources Defense Council, for example, were established. The issue begins to climb even higher in the attention of the public. Mothers against Drunk Driving was established to argue for changes in our attitudes toward drunk driving, forcing the judicial system to enforce laws punishing drunk drivers.

There are in turn spinoffs and spinoffs of organizations. There is not just one environmental organization; there are dozens. At the community level, some organizations are associated with a national organization; some are not. The EMF controversy sparked the establishment of many neighbor organizations to oppose the building of high-tension wires.

During the fourth stage the policy solutions are proposed and discussed. The issue is now fought out on the public stage. It receives attention in the national and local presses. Legislators become identified with one or the other side of the issue as the agenda is set.

Once an issue has reached the third and fourth stages, a company cannot manage the issue. It can help to define its outcome, however. But it can be done only by participating with an interest group or community organization. It has to be part of the collaborative process. Methods for working with groups are excellently described in a book called *Dealing with an Angry Public.*[16]

In the fifth stage, legislation, regulation, or practices become procedures. The issue in this sense is resolved. The Clean Air Act; the Superfund Law to require cleaning up polluted areas and its reauthorization, which mandates public reporting of chemicals used by any company producing products; a national law to increase the drinking age of minors to 21; and busing students to achieve racial balance—these are just a very few examples of legislation that came about in response to the public's concern related to issues.

In the final stage, the penalties for violating the law or practice become routine. As a consequence of the product safety legislation in 1972, for example, Firestone was required to recall, at a cost of $135 million, unsafe tires. Environmental legislation caused Exxon to be fined billions of dollars for the *Exxon Valdez* oil spill. The recall of defective products, once bitterly fought by many corporations, has become so commonly accepted that the notices appear in local newspapers weekly. A company's reputation is not faulted because of a defective product or service. Mistakes can happen. Denial of the mistake, however, does injure the credibility and trust in the company.

One way of summarizing this version of the life cycle of an issue is by saying that the expectations of yesterday become the political issues of today, the legislative requirements of tomorrow, and the litigated penalties of the day after. Over time the options available to a company for "managing" an issue narrow, whereas the consequences of penalties will increase over time, as depicted in Figure 9.2.

This is, of course, a fairly simplified depiction of the life cycle of an issue. Many issues, according to one analyst, do not go through all the stages in the life cycle.[17] The EMF case is a good example. It has peaked in the fourth stage of the life cycle and has decreased in public attention. It is unlikely that the issue, at this point, will return to the levels of public attention the issue received in the early 1990s.

Some issues get noticed and disappear before they reach the policy agenda stage. Again, the EMF issue, for example, has not been resolved. It is doubtful that it will be. Other issues occur and reoccur. Environmental issues appear to go through many different iterations of development. In some instances, solutions are not achieved, but the issue reemerges and receives increased public attention and pressure for additional solutions. Public attention to the environment was high in the 1970s and then decreased in attention until the late 1990s, when the focus of attention was on the depletion of the ozone and concern about the greenhouse effect on the environment. And there may even be new issues emerging even as one issue is being resolved.

A third pattern is the failure to achieve a legal resolution to the issue, yet it becomes accepted by default. The Three Mile Island disaster, for example, put the issue of nuclear power, once viewed as the solution to a cheap, never-ending source of energy, on the front burner of fear and concern. All across the United

Figure 9.2
Summary of Issue Life Cycle

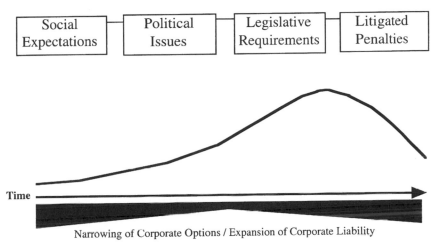

Corporate Impact on a Public Issues Life Cycle

Social Expectations	Political Issues	Legislative Requirements	Litigated Penalties

Time

Narrowing of Corporate Options / Expansion of Corporate Liability

Source: Used with the permission of Ian Wilson.

States pressure groups successfully halted nuclear power plants as an energy source. While currently no legislation exists banning the production of nuclear power plants in the United States, they are slowly disappearing, and no new ones are being built. Commonwealth Edison Company in Chicago, the United States' largest private operator of nuclear plants, for example, decided on January 15, 1998, to close two of its twelve nuclear generators because they were too expensive to operate. The company is scheduled to close two other plants; in fact, Commonwealth Edison is using only four of its twelve plants to produce electricity. Nuclear power, reported the *New York Times*, accounted for 20 percent of the nation's electricity in 1997, down from 22 percent in 1996.[18] The issue is resolving itself for the moment without a legislative solution.

Social issues, therefore, appear to go through a convoluted—not a linear—pattern of development in the reactions and counterreactions of different organizations and groups, or stakeholders, to events and their stake in the issue.[19] And the pattern is repeated when there are concerns and issues of less magnitude but of no less importance that are played out in local communities. They are often the consequences of a company's operational practices. A change in a company's operating practices, for example, may go unnoticed within the company. But it may raise issues of concern in the community.

This is a scenario based on an experience of a Massachusetts company. A new operation was introduced into the plant. It raised the noise level of operations considerably, which carried across the fenceline into the neighborhood. The residents were particularly impacted when summer arrived, and the plant left its windows opened. Residents complained, but not to the company, because they did not know to whom to complain. It was brought to the attention of the neighborhood association, a voluntary homeowners and neighborhood anticrime and watch group. The president of the association talked to the community relations manager at the company's headquarters site, who in turn notified the plant manager. A few weeks later the complaint was made again. Again the plant manager was notified.

When this brought no results, the city council representative was notified. The weekly neighborhood give-a-way newspaper wrote about it. The neighborhood association complained to the mayor; this was reported in the city newspaper and subsequently picked up in the state's largest metropolitan newspaper. The mayor, a longtime ally of the company, asked the plant manager and the community relations manager to act on the neighborhood's request for changes voluntarily. Otherwise, he explained, the city council would enact ordinances requiring expensive structures and traffic restrictions. It was now, he explained to the plant and community relations manager, out of his control.

RESPONDING TO ISSUES

As this example and the EMF case illustrate, there are lessons to be learned in understanding how concerns get expressed and in their pattern of development. It is in many ways a predictable pattern. The first step is to treat the concerns genuinely and sincerely, as early and as quickly as possible. Merck advises its managers to have "concern and sympathy for all stakeholder concerns. This is not to say that each one warrants full-scale involvement." Merck also says, "In the context of Neighbor of Choice, it is impossible to choose the best response without first developing a thorough understanding of the essential needs, concerns and issues facing the community."[20]

Second, dismissing the concerns of an individual or a community group as simplistic or the tirades of an extremist is not just foolhardy; it is also poor management. It often backfires and hardens the view of the individual or group. In the EMF controversy the individual dismissed by the company as a troublemaker reported that dismissal only emboldened him. "That got my Irish up," he claimed. He became even more emotionally involved in the issue.[21]

People who are emotionally involved in issues are tireless in their efforts to resolve them. Parents of emotionally disturbed children, for example, have overcome considerable obstacles and frustrations to bring about changes in treatment and education. The federal Education for All the Handicapped Law, for example, was enacted as a consequence of hard work organizing, educating, and lobbying elected officials on the part of parents.

Another example is the legislation to increase the legal age for purchasing alcoholic beverages. A campaign led by the Mothers against Drunk Driving was successful in including raising the drinking age across the country to 21 in the Highway Safety Act over the objections of President Ronald Reagan, as I pointed out in Chapter 1.

Third, intervene early into the development cycle of the issue. It is less onerous, less expensive, and less harmful to relationships when a company responds to a concern or issue when it first emerges—better yet, before the issue emerges.

When Merck was constructing a new plant, it discovered after meeting the neighbors that the headlights of cars exiting the planned driveway would shine into the living room of a neighbor living across from the facility. This would be a considerable nuisance during the winter months. With hardly any expense, the company changed the driveway plan.

Fourth, develop processes—community practice programs and processes—for identifying issues and concerns. Using methods for developing and sustaining relationships described in the previous chapter is one of the best ways to uncover emerging concerns. Another technique is to read the neighborhood newspapers and newsletters of community organizations.

Just knowing the concerns and issues in a community can provide ideas on how to resolve them. In Westbury, Long Island, for example, a multimillion dollar incenerator plant was built and torn down in response to the environmental concerns of the community. It was rebuilt, however, after a successful community relations program by a new owner, Re-Fuel. The company accepted, without necessarily agreeing with, the community's concerns. It involved the community in decisions on how the new incinerator would be built. Once constructed, it opened the plant for tours and receptions. Approximately 2,000 visitors tour the plant a year. It sponsors soccer tournaments and recycling contests and has distributed children's booklets on waste management.[22]

Another way of responding is to accept the inevitable. Although entrenched attitudes are difficult to overcome, often fed by fears of negative consequences by changing a course of action, it may prove necessary to change long-term policies. American automobile manufacturers, along with gasoline and coal producers, for example, depended for many years on communication strategies countering the evidence on global warming. It did not exist, they insisted. Moreover, producing non-gas-burning engines was prohibitively expensive; and in fact, investing money on research of non-gas-burning engines could bankrupt the American economy. But at the North American International Auto Show in Detroit on January 8, 1998, the three U.S. automakers announced that the fears of global warming were well founded. They were ready to produce cars using fuel cells and alternative energy sources. Ford Motor Company said that they were going to produce low-emission sports utility vehicles as early as 1999. General Motors Corporation chairman John Smith stated outright, "no car company will be able to thrive in the 21st century if it relies solely on internal combustion engines."[23]

What prompted this change from a communications to a performance issue management strategy was the results of the worldwide support of the Kyoto, Japan, environmental conference and its treaty to reduce emissions of gases harming the ozone level of the atmosphere. It was also in response to the Japanese automakers' announcement that they were moving quickly to develop low-emission cars.

In many companies, sales staffs are expected periodically to write what are called "condition letters." The condition letters are the salespersons' descriptions of the conditions of the market—changing consumer behaviors, competitors' methods, ideas for new point-of-purchase techniques, and assessment of the outlet's attitudes toward the products. They are called "letters" because they are supposed to be a brief and concise summary. This method can be copied and facility managers asked to prepare condition letters every three to six months on the issues and concerns in the community.

The Chemical Manufacturers Society advises its member companies to be aware of eight categories of community concerns, which could be used as a checklist for condition letters in any company.

1. Health
2. Safety
3. Environmental
4. Aesthetic issues
5. Equity issues
6. Cultural/symbolic issues
7. Legal/statutory issues
8. Public policy issues[24]

SUMMARY

Responding sincerely and quickly to a community's issues and concerns is the second strategy needed for a company to become a neighbor of choice. Implementing the issues and concerns strategy requires a company to develop community practice programs that respond quickly and genuinely to the concerns that will affect the company's operations.

NOTES

1. P. Brodeur, *Currents of Death: Power Lines, Computer Terminals and the Attempt to Cover Up Their Threat to Your Health* (New York: Simon & Schuster, 1989), pp. 15–24.

2. N. Wertheimer and E. Leeper, "Electrical Wiring Configurations and Childhood Cancer," *American Journal of Epidemiology*, March 1979, pp. 273–284.

3. Ibid., p. 273.

4. S. Schiefelbein, "The Invisible Threat: The Stifled Story of Electric Waves," *The Saturday Review*, September 1979, pp. 16–20.

5. P. Brodeur, *The Great Power Line Cover-Up: How the Government and the Utilities Are Trying to Hide the Cancer Hazard Posed by Electromagnetic Fields* (Boston: Little, Brown, 1993), p. 65.

6. P. Brodeur, "Annals of Radiation: The Hazards of Electromagnetic Fields, I: Power Lines," *New Yorker*, June 12, 1989, pp. 51–88; and "Annals of Radiation: Cancer and Power Lines: Calamity on Meadow Street," *New Yorker*, July 9, 1990, pp. 38–72.

7. P. Brodeur, *Currents of Death* and *The Great Power Line Cover-Up*.

8. R. L. Park, "Power Line Paranoia," *New York Times*, November 13, 1996, p. A23.

9. M. S. Linet et al., "Residential Exposure to Magnetic Fields and Acute Lymphoblastic Leukemia in Children," *New England Journal of Medicine*, Vol. 337, July 3, 1997, pp. 1–7.

10. G. Kolata, "Key Study Sees No Evidence Power Lines Cause Leukemia," *New York Times*, July 3, 1997, pp. A1, A23.

11. Quoted in W. I. Chase and T. Y. Crane, "Issue Management: Dissolving the Archaic Division between Line and Staff," in *Practical Public Affairs in an Era of Change*, ed. L. B. Dennis (New York: Public Relations Society of America and University Press of America, 1995), p. 130

12. Kolata, "Key Study Sees No Evidence," p. A23.

13. W. J. Koch and P. A. McGee, "Public Affairs and Risk Communication," in Dennis, *Practical Public Affairs*, p. 164.

14. L. Chang, "Lockheed Tax Cut May Hit Hard on High School Budget," *Sunnyvale Sun*, February 12, 1997, p. 1.

15. Interview with Jeannie Dusenberg, manager, Community Relations Lockheed Martin Missiles & Space Company, Sunnyvale, CA, March 26, 1998.

16. L. Suskind and D. Field, *Dealing with an Angry Public* (New York: Free Press, 1996).

17. H. A. Tombari, *Business and Society* (New York: Dryden Press, 1984).

18. B. J. Fedr, "Nation's Biggest Atomic Utility to Shut 2 Units," *New York Times*, January 16, 1998, p. A10.

19. J. F. Mahon, and S. A. Waddock, "Strategic Issues Management: An Integration of Issue Life Cycle Perspectives," *Business and Society*, Spring 1992, pp. 19–32.

20. Merck, *A Guide to Becoming a Neighbor of Choice* (Whitehouse Station, NJ: Merck & Co., 1997), pp. 17–18.

21. Brodeur, "Annals of Radiation: Cancer and Power Lines: Calamity on Meadow Street," p. 41.

22. J. L. Paluszek, "Public Affairs and the Community," in Dennis, *Practical Public Affairs*, p. 188.

23. Editorial, "Detroit Turns a Corner," *New York Times*, January 11, 1998, p. 18.

24. Chemical Manufacturers Association, "Risk Communication," in *The CMA Workshop Manual* (Arlington, VA: CMA, 1996).

Chapter 10

The Third Strategy: Using Community Support Programs to Build Trust

A third strategy for becoming a neighbor of choice is through the planned use of the company's community support programs—money, volunteers, and partnerships. It has not been easy to justify corporate philanthropy. At times, as I described in Chapter 3, companies have been criticized for giving stockholders' earnings to charities. But all that is in the past. Communities today expect companies to be involved in solving community problems and contributing money to improve community services. "A global economy," says Rosabeth Moss Kanter in her book *World Class,* "compels a broader conception of community and business leadership. It should not be equated simply with money, but with involvement in activities that contribute to the quality of life."[1]

Research results underscore Professor Kanter's observations. Studies conducted by the Opinion Research Corporation (ORC) found that communities attach significant importance to maintaining good relationships in communities and contributing to community charities.

An interesting sidebar to the ORC findings is that close to 60 percent of the respondents 30 years of age and under—the new generation of workers and consumers—believe that a company's responsiveness to community needs is very important. Less than half of the elderly (47 percent) believe this is impor-tant.[2]

Studies cited by two Ohio researchers buttress ORC's findings. The most effective way to demonstrate commitment to a community, found Professors Ledingham and Bruning, is through long-term support of community activities.[3]

A company's philanthropy and community support programs are also its most publicized activities in a community. They are written up in the media, publicized in company newsletters, and described in colorful brochures and pamphlets. They can generate community and even national goodwill, as witnessed by the Ronald McDonald Houses. But they can also be controversial, leading to threats of product boycotts. Antiabortion groups, as I pointed out earlier, forced AT&T to withdraw its contribution to the Planned Parenthood agency, angering millions of women. The Bank of America, Wells Fargo Company, and Levi Strauss were publicly criticized and picketed for cutting off contributions to the Boy Scouts of San Francisco because of the Scouts' refusal to admit gays as members or leaders.[4]

Community expectations along with the wide publicity given to corporate philanthropy, then, make a company's community programs an important strategy for generating community trust. There is more than one way to position the company positively and favorably in the community. To achieve that aim, however, a company's community support programs have to be planned and managed as any other important function of the business.

A caution, however, is necessary. Making charitable contributions to community organizations by itself does not necessarily gain trust. It does not give a company an added advantage when seeking community acceptance for business decisions. Disney's request for building a theme park in northern Virginia is a classic example. Another example is the community opposition to the expansion of a Merck facility in West Point, Pennsylvania, which I described in Chapter 8.

During the negotiations the leader of the opposition praised Merck's generosity to the community. He specifically cited Merck's support of the library and a little league baseball facility. But he quickly added, ''[T]hat will not influence us in continuing to oppose you on this matter.'' ''Contributions,'' now advises Merck in its *Community Relations Manual*, ''will not allow [a Merck] site to buy its way out of difficult situations.''[5] Philanthropy is no more or no less equal than each of the other two neighbor of choice strategies: relationship building and responding to community concerns and issues.

To plan and manage community support programs in ways to implement the neighbor of choice principle, a company needs to:

Determine which programs it wants to operate on its own and which it wants to outsource

Determine how much and what kind of resources it wants to expend on each of its community support programs

Determine how to make priority decisions about which programs it will support and which it will not

Determine the role of publicity in community program planning

Focus the community support programs so that they will foster relationships and build community trust

DISTINGUISHING AMONG NEEDS, PROGRAMS, AND ORGANIZATIONS TO CARRY OUT THE COMPANY'S PROGRAMS

Some companies plan, organize, and manage their own community programs. The *Washington Post*, for example, has a major focus on public education within its subscriber territory—the District of Columbia, southern Maryland, and northern Virginia. Led by its public relations director Virginia Rodriguez, the *Post* decided to design a program, organized and conducted by its public relations staff, that would both recognize the importance of school principals and provide professional development seminars on media and management training. Entitled the Distinguished Educational Leadership awards, principals are nominated for the award by teachers, students, former students, parents, administrators, or the general public. If they are selected, they are invited along with a guest to a weekend retreat at a resort, such as St. Thomas of the Virgin Islands or Puerto Rico. One day is devoted to seminars conducted by public and community relations specialists, editors and reporters, and management organizations including, for example, representatives of the Covey Leadership Center and the Boston College Center for Corporate Community Relations.

Other companies outsource all of their support of community programs. They decide on what agencies they will support and then make contributions to the agencies based on guidelines established by the company. Incidentally, the United Way, when it was first established under the name Community Chest, was the first example of corporate outsourcing of donations. Money was donated to the Community Chest, which then determined which agencies would be supported and how much each agency would receive.

Another technique is to ask community-based organizations to submit proposals for funding based on a company predesigned assessment of needs of interest to the company. It is a method of supporting nonprofit organizations used for many years by the federal government and has become popular in companies that use a foundation to administer charitable contributions. The Hitachi Foundation, for example, announces very directly in its *Annual Report*: "The Foundation does not accept unsolicited proposals." The Hitachi Foundation, as do other companies using this approach, invites nonprofit organizations to submit proposals for funding of programs or initiatives of interest to the company. The company provides a detailed description of the initiative as a guide to the nonprofit in developing its request for the proposal—usually referred to as RFP.

The company may convene, as does Hitachi, groups of grantees or nonprofits to describe and discuss their RFPs. According to Hitachi, this is "an opportunity for strategy exchange and allow[s] for a mutually reinforcing network to develop, with participants serving as both teachers and learners." It also, says Foundation chairman and former Secretary of State Elliot L. Richardson, points

out "what a good corporate citizen can do in cooperation with others to improve
the quality of life."[6]

The best way for a company to make a decision to manage and organize a
community program or outsource it is to understand the distinction between
needs, programs, and not-for-profit organizations.

Needs

Companies frequently use the term *issues* interchangeably with the concept
of community needs. Companies will say: "Our issue focus is education, or
literacy, or abused children." What they are really saying is that they are developing their charitable programs to meet a community *need*—improving education, decreasing illiteracy, or reducing child abuse.

Programs

Programs, on the other hand, are ways that communities or groups in communities respond to such needs. They establish education programs, a public
health system, transportation facilities, cultural institutions, and police, for example. Many of the programs are provided universally in the community and
supported through some form of taxation.

Others grow out of the concerns and needs of a group. They may be offered
to a special group—parochial education—and supported through voluntary
funds. Some are offered to the community as a whole but supported by a combination of gifts, fees, contributions, and taxes. Counseling services for children
and families, recreational services offered by YMCAs and YWCAs, literacy,
child abuse prevention, and art exhibits by the museum are examples.

Programs have also been developed to respond to a combination of needs. In
Minneapolis, for example, a partnership between the Minnesota Center for Arts
Education and the Minneapolis Public Schools developed a program to integrate
arts and arts-based skills into all aspects of education. The program is based on
a number of studies that suggest that when arts are part of a school curriculum,
student skills are increased, SAT scores go up, and absenteeism and dropout
rates decrease. The program is supported by the Annenberg Foundation, taxes,
and local companies.

Organizations

Not-for-profit organizations—community-based organizations—are established to carry out the programs necessary to respond to needs. Schools provide
education programs. Settlement houses may offer literacy programs. The Family
Service Agency provides counseling and child abuse prevention programs. The
Audubon Society provides education programs on the environment, to give a
few illustrations. There are specialized organizations, also. Some, for example,

are set up to respond to the financial needs of community organizations. The United Way provides a federated or combined fund-raising program for social agencies. There are, in other words, a wide and rich variety of nonprofit organizations in communities set up to carry out programs that are in response to what communities view as a social need.

While it may seem simplistic to make distinctions among needs, programs, and not-for-profit organizations, it is important for planning purposes. The one lesson that emerged from the frenzy of requests from community charities in the early 1980s was the necessity for companies to make philanthropy decisions based on planning and analysis.

A well-planned community program has to begin with a focus on a need. If the focus is on an organization, then the programs will be defined by that organization. The company's community programs, in turn, will be reactive and less likely to enhance the reputation of the company or develop broad-based community trust. Planning from a focus on needs also promotes flexibility and creativity. The Polaroid Company in Massachusetts, for example, began in the early 1980s to focus on the need to improve public education. As a high-technology company, Polaroid further narrowed its focus to improving *science* education.

The company designed a number of programs not unlike those developed at many other companies to improve science education. Teachers were given paid internships to work in the company. Employees with science background and experience were loaned to schools to support science teachers. During the planning of their programs in collaboration with educators and science teachers, Polaroid discovered that remarkably few teachers were educationally prepared to teach science. Less than 10 percent of school science teachers majored in science when in college, and some had not ever taken a science course, Polaroid learned.

This discovery prompted the company to examine alternative ways to increase the interest of trained scientists in teaching in the public schools—including the scientists employed in the development of its own products. The company's public affairs department saw an opportunity to encourage these employees when they retired to consider a career in education. To facilitate this, Polaroid developed a partnership with a nearby college to provide the necessary education courses for certification to teach in the Massachusetts schools system. Called the Bridge Program, it proved to be a popular and successful program. The program proved to be even more popular when the company began to downsize and set up early retirement programs. By focusing on a need and not a particular public school, Polaroid was able to design a program that not only was creative but also served the critical needs of public schools in Massachusetts and solved a need for the company.

By making a distinction among needs, programs, and not-for-profit organizations, a company improves the way it designs its community programs. The process begins with the identification of a need, then a study of the various types

Figure 10.1
Decision Tree for Making Decisions on Community Programs

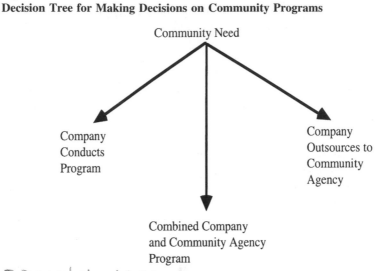

I. D a need, then study the types...

of programs that can be used or designed to meet the need. The company then makes a decision either to operate the program itself or to outsource it to a nonprofit community organization. It may also operate the program jointly or with nonprofit organizations (see Figure 10.1).

THE PROGRAM ELEMENTS OF A COMPREHENSIVE COMMUNITY SUPPORT PROGRAM

One of the dilemmas facing a company is to determine what kind of resources are needed to make a community support program effective. What are the program elements of a good community support program? A model developed by Ronald Speed when he was vice president for public affairs of Honeywell Corporation has proven to be a valuable planning tool for answering this question. First described in an article published by the Public Affairs Council,[7] the model has been modified and adapted by the Boston College Center for Corporate Community Relations. Speed arranged and described the model as containing four elements, which he depicted in the form of an inverted triangle (see Figure 10.2).

Philanthropy. At the bottom of the pyramid are the company's contributions programs—cash and in-kind gifts. They are the least important resource, but, as Speed explained, "they are significant, tangible proof of a conscious corporate decision to endorse needed community projects."

Volunteers. At the next level are "people" or the individual involvement of employees in the community activities. Employee volunteers are the most important resource of a company. Volunteers enhance and protect a company's

Figure 10.2
Comprehensive Elements of a Community Program

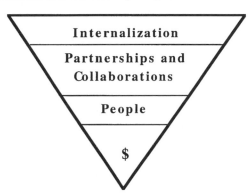

contributions. They can be used to broaden the effectiveness of a company's contributions by assisting and, if necessary, leading in carrying out the program's objectives. They help channel the energies and actions of the company in creative ways that benefit the company. They are also useful monitors of the company's contributions to an organization.

Volunteers, moreover, are the relationship builders for the company. Money does not make relationships—people do. When employees are engaged as volunteers for a company program, they become ambassadors for the company, building trust and enhancing its reputation in the community.

Employees obviously cannot be mandated to become volunteers. Nor can they be formally directed to volunteer for a program or organization that the company has selected as a company priority. Companies have discovered that they need to create an environment for voluntarism. This became particularly important during the era of downsizing in the late 1990s when employees had little time and energy to volunteer outside of their jobs. There was a feeling, too, that they were not valued by the company.

One method has been to highlight the volunteer activities of the leadership people in a company. Senior executives can provide a behavioral model for employee volunteering. Many companies also use recognition programs as incentives to encourage employee voluntarism. Some are highly imaginative, including annual appreciation dinners to luncheon with the CEO in the executive dining room.

Another very popular technique is what are called "donor incentive" programs. Employees are able to request donations, usually in the amounts of $250 to a $1,000, for a community organization in which they volunteer. This promotes volunteerism in the company and cements positive relationships with a wide variety of community organizations.

Retirees are another volunteer resource. Honeywell spearheaded this development in 1979 as a way to maintain relationships with retired employees and as a technique to gain additional volunteers for its community programs. Using retirees as volunteers for company programs has become highly popular in many companies for the very same reasons. Honeywell's program is organized and administered by retirees.

Partnerships. The third element, or as Ronald Speed termed it, "the third level of commitment," is partnerships with community agencies and organizations, and alliances with other companies. Companies that join forces with community and government organizations appear to have enhanced the effectiveness of a community program. It is a way to leverage and enhance the program.

Many companies, particularly during the early developments of business-community partnerships, became disappointed in these ventures. The problems often stemmed from too many hastily made assumptions about expectations for performance. This was particularly evident in business education partnerships. Schools expected companies to provide huge amounts of money to solve every problem. Companies held out expectations that were viewed by educators as incapable of being implemented. Companies, according to teachers, did not understand the educational environment. Not all problems could be solved immediately.

School personnel also felt demeaned and uncomfortable in their relationships with corporate managers. At a training meeting for teachers and business managers on partnership development, conducted by The Boston College Center for Corporate Community Relations, under a grant from the Edna McConnell Clark Foundation, a principal interrupted a manager who had addressed him by his first name and said: "You call me *Doctor*. And don't you forget it." His comment understandably put a chill on the discussion. Companies, on the other hand, have become impatient. As one manager explained, "A commitment we thought was made months ago never was carried out." Companies also complain that the schools only want large grants and products.

These types of problems can be overcome, however. David Herlihy, manager of the northeast facilities for IBM, for example, approached a middle school in Boston's inner city to work out a partnership that had been assigned to the company by a voluntary education commission. He began his discussion with the principal by saying, "I don't have any money for contributions. And we have no computers to give you. But we have some very talented volunteers and a commitment to making a partnership with your school work. How should we begin?"

After the principal got over his initial shock, the two began a dialogue. They discovered, first, that they liked each other. Their discussions led to an establishment of respect and trust. Out of the trust grew a relationship. Employee volunteers came to the school and became engaged in mentoring students, lecturing about the business world, helping the administrators develop better management skills, and designing easier management tools. Grants and gifts of computers shortly followed. The cash and the computers were put to use as a consequence of the mutual planning between the company and the community.

It was a successful partnership. The school and the company were singled out by the Boston school system as an example of how school-business partnerships could work. The principal and the IBM manager became a traveling team, speaking at seminars and institutes of businesses and schools.

The lesson of this partnership is the need to establish trusting relationships at the outset. Part of that trust is being clear about both the school's and the company's expectations—both the explicit and implicit expectations. It is critical to the success of any partnership that attempts be made to make explicit the unwritten expectations and hidden agendas. They should be part of the negotiations for the establishment of the partnership. If the unwritten expectations or hidden agenda items are not negotiated, the partnership will be ineffectual and become a partnership in name only.

Another form of partnership is an alliance with other companies to take advantage of the individual resources of each of the companies. Professional athletes, for example, have a unique and commanding resource. They are charismatic and able to capture the attention of youngsters. On the other hand athletes are employed by sports teams with limited staff. The average NBA (National Basketball Association) basketball team, for example, has fewer than two dozen employees and even fewer ballplayers. By joining with another company with a larger number of employees, however, a basketball team is able to maximize its efforts. The NBA, for example, collaborated with IBM facilities in a number of cities in a joint educational effort. The players' publicity value was useful in publicizing the attention to an educational program, and IBM was able to provide large numbers of volunteers to carry out the program.

Internalization. At the top of the inverted pyramid is the institutionalization, or internalization, of the community program into the values of the company. The aim is to incorporate the external commitments inside the company in such a way as to ensure that company decisions and policies work toward solving community problems. "Responsibility," as Speed insists, "starts at home."

A company internalizes its commitment to a program in many ways. For example, a company may determine that it wants to develop a focus on public education. It contributes money and products to the program, facilitates and encourages with incentives for employee volunteers, and enters into a partnership with a community school to make it a fully comprehensive program. How does the company demonstrate its commitment to the educational initiative? One way companies are showing their commitment to employees is to allow employees time off to attend parent-teacher conferences. Another way is for the CEO to take a public stance on the issue. Louis Gerstner, CEO of IBM, for example, has publicized the company's commitment to improving education. He has also written a book—*Reinventing Education*[8]—describing his commitment and ways for improving education in the United States.

A still further way is to make expectations for senior officer involvement in the focused community programs of the company. When Craig Sullivan became president and CEO of the Clorox Company in 1993, he explained to his executive committee that community involvement was an important value and business goal for the company. In August 1994, he went further and stated that all officers should be involved on boards of community agencies in the headquarters site—Oakland, California. Three years later, August 1997, he announced to his executive committee a still further goal of community commitment: Every officer in the company needed to be involved in the focus programs of the company—education and youth services. Sullivan expects this goal to be fully realized in three years.

Honeywell developed a program on the disabled and demonstrated its commitment to the program by ensuring there was full and available access for the disabled (this was well before the passage of the federal legislation mandating access).

In other words, the workplace becomes the place to demonstrate the company's commitment to working on solutions to societal and community issues. This enhances the value of the program in and outside the company. Ron Speed's model has been adapted by many companies because of its simplicity and effectiveness. It has substantially contributed to the success of Honeywell's much admired community relations programs.

FOCUSED PROGRAMS AND DISCRETIONARY PROGRAMS

While Speed's model is a very effective and successful way to design a community support program, it presents a formidable dilemma: A company cannot deploy those kinds of resources to all its programs and organizations. It isn't possible. Moreover, there are requests from some organizations that are simply not going to be funded. They do not meet guidelines. Or they are far outside the interest or so-called community focus of the company

Despite attempts at prioritizing and focusing support to a limited number of agencies, companies are still asked to support agencies that are well outside the agreed-upon focus. It may be a one-shot request to meet the capital needs of an agency building campaign. Or it is a number of requests from small charities that provide services that are important to a community's quality of life—the volunteer fire service, the library, the historical society, an arts and craft museum, for example.

Other examples include a cause-related marketing effort promoted by the company's marketing department, designed purely to increase the sale of products. It may be programs of direct interest to the CEO, such as a charity dinner, a testimonial dinner for other CEOs, or a charity golf tournament. There could also be requests for a pet charity of a board member, vendor, or purchaser. All of these may well be outside the company's major focus of interest.

Some of the requests for support are made through the company's organized channels and according to the company's guidelines and policies. Others may be informal: a telephone request from a board member; a note from the CEO or other officer in the company; an e-mail from an employee on behalf of a community organization; an invitation to support a testimonial for a leading and influential community citizen; a letter from one of the company's major consumers; or a call from the CEO's wife or husband. There are any number of ways, some quite imaginative, by which requests get funneled into a company. Few of them can be ignored, particularly those from substantial consumers or the CEO.

Community relations and corporate foundation managers are frustrated, and at times angered, at spending time responding or acceding to programs peripheral to the company's planned focus they designed. Yet it is difficult—and in fact impractical—to refuse to support such organizations because they are outside of the company's focus. To set such a limit would alienate individuals and organizations in the community or employees in the company and possibly damage the reputation and trust that the company is trying to build.

One way to handle this issue is to make a distinction among programs that are a priority or focus of the company, those that can be defined as marginal or peripheral to the focus, and those in which there is a uniform consensus that they are beyond the company's interest or concern. The priority programs can be called *signature* programs. These are selected to command the major planning, resources, and company time and effort. Often, they are limited in number to three or four a year. They are reviewed annually to determine if they will continue as a focus in succeeding years.

Building trust and meeting a company's business needs (next chapter) should be the major criteria for the selection of signature programs. These criteria should also guide the selection of community organizations chosen to carry out the program.

Focused programs should be comprehensive in scope, contain all four of the Speed program elements, and be given resources from all the major functions and departments in the company. These programs should be considered integral to the operation of the business and a necessary and essential part of the company's value chain, as explained in Chapter 3.

Signature programs can be—and very often are—planned, organized, and carried out by the company, not necessarily as just contributions to a community organization or agency. The *Washington Post* Distinguished Educational Leadership program is an example. Clorox's emphasis on education and youth services in Oakland is another example.

Signature programs can also take the form of direct contributions to an agency. Many companies, for example, consider their support of the United Way a signature program. Frequently, companies do not limit their support to the annual contribution. They publicize the United Way in the company, organize and support an employee campaign for contributions, loan staff and executives to assist the United Way, and encourage executives to serve in leadership roles for the community United Way and the national United Way of America. This type of support from a company can be very substantial.

Discretionary programs are those that as a consequence of the company's study and analysis fall below the priority level of signature programs. They are exclusively in the form of cash or in-kind contributions to not-for-profit organizations or agencies. Decisions are made annually. A company does not consider these requests as unimportant. They do not merit, however, all the time and effort necessary to develop a comprehensive and focused signature program, and thus are categorized as discretionary requests.

While it is preferable that any community program build trust and contribute to its competitive advantage, these are not essential criteria for discretionary programs. But they should not cause the trust quotient to be diminished or lead to hindering the competitive advantage of the company. At the very least, they should be neutral.

To avoid contributing to organizations that could give a negative reputation to the company, carefully designed guidelines or criteria are needed. Some suggested questions that should be asked before a contribution is made to a not-for-profit organization are listed in Figure 10.3.

Making a distinction between signature and discretionary programs has obvious advantages. It allows a company to use its resources more effectively. Staff is able to focus on a limited number of programs that can benefit the company and the community while still being able to respond to unique issues. Another advantage, which is particularly useful for companies with many different sites, is to be able to design a signature program that is a focus for the entire company and allows nonheadquartered sites to design variations of their own discretionary programs. IBM's corporate focus is education. Louis Gerstner, IBM's CEO, has devoted a significant amount of resources—financial and human—to improving public education. He brought on to the community relations staff people whose background is in public education. While IBM sites around the world have to support and work on the education focus, they are encouraged and expected to develop programs specific and unique to their own communities.

The National Basketball Association designed an education program that would focus on encouraging youngsters to stay in school and complete their education. The "Stay in School" program was initiated in 1990. All the NBA teams were encouraged to support the program during the year and to conduct a highly publicized "Stay in School" jamboree at one of the games during the week of the NBA All-Star game.

The League office provided publicity and planning material for each of the teams. It also conducted, in collaboration with a team, its own jamboree for students each year in the city where the All-Star game is played. Staff from the League office is loaned to the All-Star site community to work with the local team's community relations staff. The staff, along with the players, visits the schools and discusses with students the importance of completing their education. Youngsters from the community who have perfect attendance for four

Figure 10.3
Criteria Questions for Making Decisions on the Support of Not-for-Profit Organizations

Does the organization meet legal and statutory requirements of a not-for-profit, thus allowing for gifts to be tax deductible?

Does the organization fulfill a genuine community or societal need?

Is the organization managed according to professional standards, and does it adhere to the operating standards of its own profession?

Does the organization have the leadership (volunteer and professional) to carry out any programs that might be supported by the company?

Does it have an active board or committee overseeing the activities of the organization?

Does the organization publish an annual report including an audited account of its income and expenses as well as an audit of *for-profit* subsidiaries?

Are there provisions, either through election or by limitation, in the terms of membership to allow for rotation of board membership?

What is the reputation of the organization in carrying out its current mission and role?

Does the organization have sufficient human and financial resources to carry out its present programs and functions?

Is the organization respected and trusted by its clients and key opinion leaders and other companies in the community?

Does the organization fully understand the scope and objectives of the program that it will undertake on behalf of the company?

Can it obtain additional resources if necessary to carry out the program?

Will the organization promote and facilitate the development of positive relationships for the company in the community?

Will the organization enhance the reputation of the company in the community?

Is the organization likely to harm the company's reputation in the community?

months are invited to an event on the Saturday morning prior to the All-Star game. They meet the players and are entertained by rock groups and celebrities.

Each of the teams develops its own signature and discretionary programs. They all, however, work with the League office to support a national program in collaboration with each other. This provides a unified and nationally publicized effort but still permits teams to respond to the unique needs of their local communities.

Another advantage of discretionary programs is that they can be used to pretest signature programs. A company can explore the opportunities for the development of a comprehensive program by first making a contribution to a not-for-profit organization. The company can then evaluate the work of the organization as well as the feasibility and advisability of establishing working relationships.

PUBLICIZING COMMUNITY SUPPORT PROGRAMS

Generating publicity of company contributions to communities has been a subject of controversy as well as concern. About 20 or 30 years ago, companies were very reluctant to publicize their contributions to the community for fear of stimulating more requests for money from community agencies. "Do good—but don't let anyone know about it" was the admonition of CEOs.

The Reagan initiatives for more community involvement caused a rethinking of this philosophy. Pressures were put on companies to become involved, and companies needed to let the community know they were involved. Many companies, particularly those with long histories of supporting community agencies and ventures, were still reluctant to advertise their good works. "Do good—and let's hope we get caught at it" became a revised catchphrase.

As evidence that a company's community involvement can influence public, consumer, and employee attitudes began to grow, newer thoughts were given to advertising good works. If consumers were more willing to buy products from companies that were involved, then it was good marketing sense to publicize what the company was doing. If employees are influenced by the company's community reputation, then it is prudent to let the employees know what the company is doing. And if the community is more tolerant, forgiving, and supportive of companies with a community record, they, too, should know about the company's programs. Now the message is: "Do good—and make sure we are caught at it!"

Given the new attitudes toward corporate community involvement, there is no reason for a company not to publicize its programs and activities. In fact, publicity should be an integral part of the community program strategy.

Studies support the necessity of communication for community programs. "In one midwestern area," according to Professors Ledingham and Bruning, "an organization invested millions of dollars in the community with no apparent impact on public loyalty. However, loyalty ratings improved significantly after the organization conducted an informational campaign that emphasized its investment."[9] A communications strategy, therefore, needs to be part of a company's community program planning. But it needs to be done within a context—a context of building trust. The message cannot be so self-serving that it creates antagonism and mistrust. The reason for publicizing what the company does in a community is to enhance its reputation. Merck describes its reason in this way: "If we don't let our communities know about our integrity and our ability, then we haven't allowed them to evaluate our operations. When that happens we forfeit an opportunity to deepen our relationships of trust."[10]

USING COMMUNITY SUPPORT PROGRAMS TO BUILD TRUST

Trust needs to be the essential goal of any company's community support program if it wants to become a neighbor of choice. The programs have to be able to contribute to developing the company's legacy of trust in the community. In that sense, they can be likened to what Virginia Rodriguez of the *Washington Post* calls "a community insurance program."

To determine if a community support program provides insurance for building trust, it should be evaluated against three questions:

Does the program contribute to developing positive and sustainable relationships?

Does the program respond to the community's concerns and needs?

Does the program contribute to sustaining or improving the quality of life in the community?

One way to build trust is in the design of the program itself, an example of which is the *Washington Post*'s educational program described earlier. Each year the principals who are nominated for the Distinguished Educational Leadership Award are announced at a dinner to which those who nominated the winning principals are also invited. One of the nominators, a member of the Alexandria (Virginia) City Council who attended the 1997 dinner, wrote a letter of praise to the publisher of the *Post*, Donald Graham. In his letter the council member said, "Your paper doesn't always get it right. But you got it exactly right last night with the Distinguished Educational Leadership Awards program."[11] While it appears that the *Post* as a newspaper may have lost the Council member's trust, the *Post* educational program has been able to add to the Post Company's community trust account.

Another way to build trust is to involve representatives of the community in guiding and selecting the company's community support programs. This is done by obtaining information on the quality-of-life needs of a community directly from community residents. This kind of information can be obtained through the informal relationships that are established by community relations or foundation staff or through periodic needs assessment surveys and interviews, such as those described in Chapter 7.

A series of questions need to be asked that reveal the relative importance of specific community needs. An example of a few questions, with general instructions, is contained in Figure 10.4. The responses are scaled for the purpose of analysis and comparison. It is not uncommon also to ask the respondents to identify, in order of priority, the three top needs in the community. Nor is it uncommon to ask what kinds of needs the company should focus on in its community programs.

It is important to preface a community needs assessment with the comment

Figure 10.4
Sample of Questions and Instructions Used in a Community Needs Assessment

---

Priority Needs in Our Community

We are now interested in your opinion about the importance of social and health needs in our community. Please answer the questions in terms of how important a need this is in our community. A response of 1 means that you feel this is not an important need. A response of 5 means that you feel it is very important, and a response of 3 means that it is between somewhat important and somewhat not important.

QUESTION	RESPONSES				
Improving public education	1	2	3	4	5
Providing recreational facilities	1	2	3	4	5
Reducing drug and other substance abuses	1	2	3	4	5
Providing facilities for victims of family abuse	1	2	3	4	5
Maintaining a clean environment	1	2	3	4	5
Improving transportation facilities	1	2	3	4	5

---

that the company cannot meet all the needs of the community and that the purpose of the assessment is to assist the company in developing a more focused set of programs to meet the needs of the community as best as it can.

The needs assessment not only helps in establishing priorities for a company, but it is also a signaling technique. It announces to the community that the company is serious and caring in its efforts—that it is involving the community in its program decisions.

An example of a summary of responses to a community needs assessment conducted by Boston College Center for Corporate Community Relations is shown in Figure 10.5. The respondents to this needs assessment believed that the most critical needs facing their community were improving public education (K–12), maintaining a clean environment, reducing crime, and reducing drug abuse. A company that designed its community support programs for any of these four needs would be able to justify and publicize its decisions as a genuine response to a need defined by the community.

SUMMARY

Planning community support programs requires considerable time and energy. Because of its publicity implications, a company cannot leave these decisions to chance. Furthermore, community support programs offer a company significant opportunities to build a legacy of trust in a community. They have a major effect on how a company is viewed in the community. If community members are involved as advisers in the company's decision making, their participation promotes trust and relationships of trust.

Figure 10.5
Example of Average of Responses to Community Needs Assessment

Need	Score
Improving education	4.8
Reducing crime	4.5
Supporting arts and culture	2.1
Cleaning the environment	4.7
Reducing illiteracy	3.1
Supporting higher education	2.3
Reducing drug abuse	4.0
Improving race relations	3.8
Reducing homelessness	3.5
Reducing traffic congestion	3.0

1 = not important; 5 = very important.

NOTES

1. R. M. Kanter, *World Class: Thriving Locally in the Global Economy* (New York: Simon & Schuster, 1995), p. 197.

2. B. C. O'Hare, "Good Deeds Are Good Business," *American Demographics Magazine*, September 1991, pp. 33–42.

3. J. A. Ledingham and S. D. Bruning, "Building Loyalty through Community Relations," *Public Relations Strategist*, Vol. 2, no. 2, September 1997, pp. 27–29.

4. M. Ewell, "Firms' Scout Cutoff Criticized," *Boston Globe*, August 8, 1992.

5. Merck, *A Guide To Becoming a Neighbor of Choice* (Whitehouse Station, NJ: Merck & Co., 1997), p. 25.

6. D. A. Roy, "From the President," in *From People to Partnerships, 1996 Annual Report* (Washington, D.C.: Hitachi Foundation, 1996), p. 4.

7. Ronald Speed first described this in an article for the Public Affairs Council. R. K. Speed, "Throwing Money at Community Problems Isn't All There Is to Corporate Responsibility, *Public Affairs Review*, 1984, pp. 48–53. He later revised the categories in sessions he led for the Center for Corporate Community Relations at Boston College between 1985 and 1989.

8. L. V. Gerstner, R. D. Semerad, D. P. Doyle, and W. B. Johnston, *Reinventing Education: Entrepreneurship in America's Public Schools* (New York: Dutton, 1994).

9. Ledingham and Bruning, "Building Loyalty," p. 29.

10. Merck, *A Guide to Becoming a Neighbor of Choice*, p. 12.

11. V. Rodriguez, interview with author March 17, 1998.

Chapter 11

. . . And Achieve a Competitive Advantage

While I have stressed repeatedly that the primary goal of a company's community support programs is to promote trust and build relationships, there are a number of very good reasons why a company would want to take advantage of the opportunity to use its community support programs to achieve its own business strategies and goals.

First, a company is more likely to get the support of its senior managers if its community programs take into account its short- and long-term economic interests. They will want to ensure that the programs are successful. Time Warner, for example, has designed a huge literacy program called "Time to Read," because it knows its long-term interests depend on a reading public. This convinces management that the program is not merely a contribution to the community but a part of its economic success.

Second, when a company tailors its community support programs to its specific business goals, it is able to exploit its own resources and unique strengths. It can develop better and more effective community programs. Moreover, employees are more willing to volunteer for community activities that enable them to use their knowledge, experience, and skills. High-tech companies, for example, are able to leverage the technical skills of employees in working with students on science projects.

Third, it supports the basic business reasons of the company. As Michael Porter maintains, "*Everything* [his emphasis] a firm does should be captured in a primary or support activity [of a company's value chain]."[1]

Fourth, it makes strategic sense to take advantage of opportunities to improve growing a business with an activity that a company has to do anyway. Successful companies seek opportunities for every activity.

A company, therefore, should factor in its business needs and goals when it

makes decisions on the kinds of community support programs it will develop
or the organizations in the community it will support. There are three ways that
this can be done. One way is to use needs assessments techniques to identify
the community service needs of a company and then match them with the community's opinions of its needs. A second way is to evaluate the direct benefits
that can be achieved by the company by supporting a community organization.
And a third way is to use competitive strategies as a guide for designing and
supporting community organizations.

MATCHING COMPANY AND COMMUNITY NEEDS

Companies depend on many services in a community to achieve business
goals. They need, to cite just a few examples,

An educationally prepared workforce

A safe and secure work and home environment for their employees and their families

Child and adult day care services for working parents

Recreational facilities for employees and families

Adequate transportation system

A community free of discord and animosity

Cultural facilities to enhance and broaden community life

If these services are not adequate or available, a company can provide them
itself or improve existing services, or both. Some companies, for example, offer
child day care services for employees and contribute money to community day
care services. Companies operate their own training programs and support
schools at the same time.

One of the most effective ways to assess the adequacy of community services
needed to meet company objectives is to conduct an internal needs assessment.
In this process managers are interviewed for their opinions on the adequacy and
availability of community services that are needed for them to achieve their
function's business goals. How critical, for example, is the community's educational system in preparing the current and future workforce? Similar questions
are asked about all other community services (see Figure 11.1).

The responses are scaled for the purpose of analysis and comparison. It is not
uncommon to also ask the respondents to identify, in order of priority, the three
top needs in the community. A sample of all employees should be surveyed to
obtain their opinions about the quality-of-life needs in the community. The instrument used should be the same as that used in conducting a community needs
assessment (see Figure 10.4).

Figure 11.2 is an example of the results of an assessment conducted by the
Boston College Center for Corporate Community Relations. With little variation,
these results are quite common. For some companies, those in oil, chemical, or

Figure 11.1
Sample of Questions and Instructions Used in a Company Needs Assessment

---

Priority Needs in Our Community

We are now interested in your opinion about the importance of community services on achieving the goals of your function. Please answer the questions in terms of the availability or adequacy of services that may be obstacles to achieving your function's strategies and goals. A response of 1 means that this is not a critical obstacle. A response of 5 means that you feel it is very critical, and a response of 3 means that it is in between somewhat critical and somewhat not critical. If you do not know the answer circle the DK response.

QUESTION			RESPONSES			
Improving public education	1	2	3	4	5	DK
Providing recreational facilities	1	2	3	4	5	DK
Reducing drug and other substance abuses	1	2	3	4	5	DK
Providing facilities for victims of family abuse	1	2	3	4	5	DK
Maintaining a clean environment	1	2	3	4	5	DK
Improving transportation facilities	1	2	3	4	5	DK

---

pharmaceutical industries, environment may be ranked higher. In the publishing industries, literacy is often ranked among the top three or four. And in the high-tech industry, higher education is often ranked in the top tier of needs. The appearance of "workforce diversity" on the list is not uncommon. When interviewed, managers frequently view this as a community problem that becomes a need for the company to solve.

By comparing the company's assessment of needs, with the community's assessment of needs, a company is able to design or support programs that meet the needs of both the company and the community (see Figure 11.3). The ranking provides guidance in priority setting of community programs meeting both the company's and the community's assessment of needs. A company examining these scores would want to design or support its major programs that focus on education, crime, and environment.

Another way to depict the relationship between the company's and the community's assessment is to use a matrix as a planning guide (Figure 11.4). The comparison of the findings on a matrix serves two useful purposes. One, it helps in setting priorities for program planning. It also reveals a number of planning challenges. It is apparent, for example, that there is clearly a consensus that education is a critical need for both the company and the community. On the other hand, there is disagreement about the importance of arts and culture. Companies tend to give importance to arts and culture because it is a means of providing an attractive quality of life for its managers. Community residents may rank the issue low in comparison to other issues deemed of more importance. A company may decide to support arts and cultural organizations but not

Figures 11.2
Example of Average of Responses to Company Needs Assessment

Need	Score
Education (K–12)	4.9
Crime	4.8
Arts and culture	4.5
Workforce diversity	4.1
Environment	3.9
Literacy	3.8
Higher education	3.3
Substance abuse	2.9
Race relations	2.1
Homelessness	1.5
Traffic	1.4

1 = not important; 5 = very important.

Figure 11.3
Example of Average of Responses to Company and Community Needs Assessments

Need	Company Score	Community Score
Education (K–12)	4.9	4.8
Crime	4.8	4.5
Arts and culture	4.5	2.1
Workforce diversity	4.1	—
Environment	3.9	4.7
Literacy	3.8	3.1
Higher education	3.3	2.1
Substance abuse	2.9	4.0
Race relations	2.1	3.8
Homelessness	1.5	3.5
Traffic	1.4	3.0

1 = not important; 5 = very important.

Figure 11.4
Comparison of Company and Community Needs Assessments

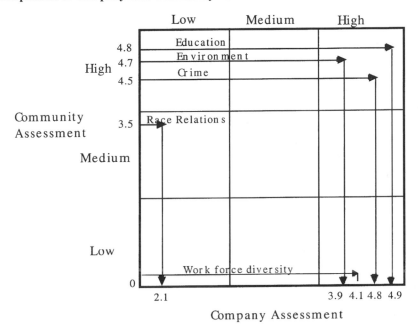

Company Assessment

as a priority or signature program. A case could also be made for responding similarly to the needs of literacy, higher education, and substance abuse.

Two, a company can redefine needs to meet both company and community concerns. The company's respondents, for example, consider diversity to be a critical social issue to the company's future (a ranking of 4.8). This is an issue that has current and long-term implications for many companies. On the other hand, the community does not even identify workforce diversity, because it is a business issue. It does rank race relations, however, as an important need (3.5). A company can creatively combine the two perspectives and develop program options that promote improved race relations in the community with diversity experiences and training for its employees. In turn, the company can select organizations such as the NAACP, the Urban League, or even a school in an inner-city neighborhood to carry out the program. As we noted earlier, companies such as UPS and Thom McAn have developed programs for just these purposes.

The matrix depiction is also a very useful way to describe a company's program decisions to managers and community residents.

ASSESSING THE VALUE OF COMMUNITY SUPPORT PROGRAMS TO THE COMPANY

The second way to make decisions about what kinds of community organizations the company wants to support is to do it on the basis of benefits that a company can accrue. Pioneered by Alan Smithers and Chris Marsden for the British Petroleum (BP) Company, the "value assessment process," as they call it, has been used by BP to decide the level of support it wants to give to individual educational partnerships.[2]

The premise behind BP's approach, according to company managing director and chief executive Russell Seal, is that its educational programs are "not a charitable activity but a business tool for enhancing our reputation and license to operate." The programs, therefore, should be operated "in a quality, businesslike way with clear benefits (i.e. objectives) sought, achieved and evaluated."[3]

The techniques BP uses are no different than what it uses to assess the competitive value of all its business. By comparing the relative attractiveness of a business unit in an industry and the strength or competitive position of the unit, the company is able to decide, for example, which business units it may want to improve and which it may want to get rid of. Developed by General Electric, McKinsey and Company, and Shell and called *portfolio analysis*, it is a technique widely used by companies to design competitive strategies.[4]

In applying portfolio analysis to its assessment of its education partnerships, the company asks two questions: What are we seeking for the company? What are we seeking for the educational partnership? To determine the benefits to the company, BP uses a ranking of five additional questions or objectives:

1. Will the educational program contribute to the motivation and development of BP's staff?
2. Will the educational program create opportunities for the company to understand, influence, and learn from education?
3. Will the educational program help the company to recruit employees both in the long and short term?
4. Will the educational program earn the company goodwill?
5. Will the educational program give access to resources (teachers, students, etc.) for the company?

To determine the benefits of the partnership to the education program, the following five questions are asked:

1. Will the educational program contribute to the motivation and development of the staff and students?
2. Will the educational program create opportunities to understand, influence, and learn from the company?

Figure 11.5
Impacts of BP's Educational Programs

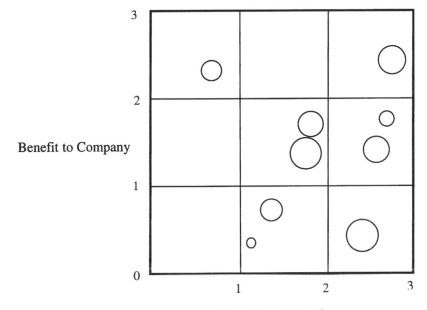

Benefit to Education

Source: Used with the permission of C. Marsden.

3. Will the educational program help students make informed career choices?

4. Will the educational program earn the school goodwill?

5. Will the educational program give the school access to the resources of other companies and organizations?

The analysis of the questions is conducted by BP managers. To assist, teachers who have been on loan to BP may also be involved. Approximately ten people in all participate in the analysis. BP obtains a ranking to the statements on a scale of 1 to 5, with 5 being given to the objective considered most important and 1 to the objective regarded as the least important. It next develops a product score. Since there are five items carrying a total of 15 ranking points, the product score can range anywhere from 15 to 75. A score is obtained for both the benefits to the company and the benefits to education.

Costs are then attributed to the particular school business program. These are estimates based on the company's experience in budgeting other programs.[5] The results are transferred to a matrix for discussion and decision (Figure 11.5). Each of the circles represents a partnership educational program operated by one of BP's companies. The size of the circles represents cost of the programs.

Those programs that are positioned in or near the upper-right-hand quadrant are judged to provide greater benefits to the company and the education partnership.[6] Decisions could range from investing further in a particular program to shutting it down. It also can point to areas where improvements can be made to add to the benefits to the company and the educational partnership.

The BP benefits approach offers a number of distinct advantages. First, it is based on business practices that are used by many companies in making business strategy decisions. Consequently, it is a familiar analytical tool that is thus readily accepted by managers.

Second, it lends itself to developing methods for adding more precise measures to assessments. Market research tools and reputational analysis methods can be used to strengthen the assessments. Consequently, it can strengthen research into evaluating the results of a partnership or any type of association with a community organization.

Third, it is a method that can easily be used by both business and education participants. BP explains that it takes only a day to conduct the analysis with the participants from the education system.

Since publication of the original results of the BP value assessment, some interesting changes have been made. Company and education representatives engage in a brainstorming session to analyze the benefits of the program. In fact, Chris Marsden, formerly of BP and now a faculty member of the Warwick Business School, reports that the brainstorming session is vital to learning and relationship building. A real test of the success of a partnership, according to Marsden, "is when each side, particularly from education, understand for the first time what the real benefits being sought by the other side are and take responsibility for achieving them."

Moreover, reports Marsden, the value assessment is being used by accounting firms in developing a computerized assessment process for measuring corporate social performance.[7]

SUSTAINING A COMPETITIVE ADVANTAGE THROUGH THE USE OF COMMUNITY SUPPORT PROGRAMS

A third approach combines elements of the other two and uses competitive strategy as the criterion for setting priorities. The focus is on an analysis of the programs or organizations the company is supporting, not on community needs. Each program is analyzed on the basis of its contribution to sustaining the company's competitive advantage.

Based on the work of Michael Porter,[8] two key questions are asked about any community program:

Does the program help the company become a cost leader?

Does the program help the company differentiate its products in the marketplace?

For some companies, cost leadership may be the overriding strategy. A manufacturing company, for example, in a highly competitive industry may want to base its decisions on how much the program will help it to reduce costs. Often, these are human resource costs: costs of recruiting a qualified workforce and reducing training costs, for example.

Others, consumer-focused companies as an example, may emphasize strategies that help to differentiate their products. Cause marketing, as we saw in Chapter 3, is a way to differentiate a product. Another way is in the selection of the type of program support. For years Texaco has supported the Metropolitan Opera on radio to differentiate the company as a superior organization. Mobil Corporation is a major and longtime contributor to artistic and cultural programs, which it calls "pragmatic altruism."

And still others may combine the two competitive strategies. Hewlett Packard, for example, has supported science education as a means to increase skilled technicians. As it moves more and more into the consumer market with its printers and computers, it publicizes its community program activities to differentiate itself with computer consumers.

To provide an illustration of how a company can analyze the competitive strengths of its community support programs, let us examine the contributions program of a hypothetical manufacturing company in a headquarters city. The company is contributing to the support of nine nonprofit organizations. For some the support is in the form of money only. For others it includes money, products, and volunteers. For one organization, a school, the company has also developed a partnership. The programs/organizations that the company has been supporting are the following:

1. Youth delinquency prevention program at the Carey Settlement House, which is located in a neighborhood near the firm's manufacturing facility. The goal of the program is to reduce vandalism in the neighborhood.

2. A partnership with Alexander Middle School. It focuses on improving math and reading skills. The company also supports and encourages an employee mentoring program in the school.

3. United Way. Company makes a significant contribution to the United Way (45 percent of total of the company's contribution budget). The United Way is the federated fund-raising organization supporting the operating costs of most of the community's social services and recreation agencies, such as family counseling agencies, YMCA and YWCA, child guidance agency, Boy and Girl Scouts, Catholic Charities, Salvation Army, neighborhood settlement houses, and Boys and Girls Clubs. The company also supports the agency by conducting an intensive employee fund-raising drive called "Day of Caring." It also loans two executives and a secretary for three months to United Way during the drive.

4. Contributes 10 percent of contributions budget to city's Children's Cancer Center.

5. Half a dozen dinners annually on behalf of local charities honoring other CEOs or local celebrities to which the company donates $700 to $1,500 to each.

6. Charity golf tournament on behalf of a national boys' recreation agency. Company is a participating sponsor and contributes $150,000 each year.

7. National children's disability organization, which is supported through a cause-related marketing program effort for one of the firm's consumer products.

8. Allston Community Library. Makes annual contribution representing 5 percent of contribution budget. The company has been a supporter of this organization since its founding.

9. A state park and recreational facility in the county. Company is a major sponsor of programs that maintain environmental cleanliness of the park. Company uses this event also to promote team building and morale among employees. Employees and their families, including the CEO, are invited to a weekend that involves cleaning up and repairing and painting cabins and recreational areas. It is an event that is looked forward to by many employees.

We can arrange these community contributions programs along a continuum from those that contribute highly to either one or both of Porter's core competitive strategies to those that make little or no contribution. For example, those that can contribute significantly to the company's competitive advantage could be:

The youth delinquency project at Carey Settlement House under the assumption that costs of repairing facilities because of vandalism and theft of property would be reduced. In addition, reduced vandalism would make employees feel safe coming to and from the facility. This would be an aid in recruiting employees.

The Alexander Middle School project with its goal to improve the readiness of students for employment with the company. This saves training costs for the company.

The state park clean-up program. This contributes to facilitating the company's human resource strategies. It promotes team building, improves employee morale by involving families in a community/business effort, and aids in recruiting and retaining employees.

The cause-related marketing program, which is designed specifically to increase sales of a product. This helps to differentiate the company's products and increase sales.

Those organizations that make a medium contribution to the competitive strategies could be:

The Children's Cancer Center program, which might aid in the differentiating strategy, but it would need to be advertised.

Similar to the Children's Cancer Center program, Allston Library support may assist in a differentiating strategy, but the costs of any extensive support of the organization may be outweighed by the results.

The United Way, which often receives the lion's share of most companies' contributions programs as well as the volunteer support of many managers, gets discounted as a competitive advantage because the contributions and efforts get lost in the highly publicized contributions from all other companies and individuals. The frequent complaint of many

Figure 11.6
Impact of Community Program on Competitive Advantage Strategies (Low Cost/Product Differentiation)

COMPETITIVE ADVANTAGE

High	Carey Settlement House Alexander School State park Cause marketing project
Medium	United Way Children's Cancer Agency Allston Library
Low	Charity dinners Golf tournament

companies is that they get little or no recognition for their support of the United Way. The United Way funding of some agencies and services, however, saves costs for companies.[9]

Those organizations that would contribute very little to the competitive advantage of the company are the golf tournament and the charity dinners.

Figure 11.6 can be used to graphically depict the distribution of the company's community contribution programs and their benefit as a competitive strategy. Using competitive advantage as a strategy, the company can decide that its focused or signature programs will be those that support the organizations in the top cell. Those in the medium or low cells can be classified as discretionary programs to which the company may make donations but will not necessarily provide employee volunteer support or enter into any partnership arrangement. In fact, this analysis may provide an argument for discontinuing support to organizations in the lowest cell.

MATCHING COMPETITIVE ADVANTAGE WITH A STRATEGY OF BUILDING TRUST

But this only accounts for one half of the analysis. Programs a company supports should also contribute to building trust in the community. One measure of trust is the community's assessment of its needs. Programs a company designs or supports that respond to what the community identifies as its most important needs are likely to enhance community trust. They are also likely to increase relationships with key organizations and leaders in the community.

The responses to the community needs assessment described in the last chapter, which are fairly typical of responses to needs assessments, can be used as a basis for determining levels of trust. Using the same organizations of the previous example, they can be arranged along a dimension of high trust to low trust.

The programs that could contribute to high trust:

The Alexander Middle School doubtlessly responds to the high concern that communities have about the quality of their schools.

The Carey Settlement House project reflects probably the concerns and fears of residents about vandalism. It is also an agency within the fenceline community of the company and one with which the company needs to have positive and favorable relationships.

The state park program is designed to respond to the environmental concerns of community residents.

Because of its unique capacity to involve key individuals in a community in its organization, the United Way provides networking and relationship building opportunities.

Programs that contribute to medium trust:

The Allston Library, because it is generally not ranked highly by community residents as an important need
The Children's Cancer Center, also not highly ranked

Programs that would likely contribute very little to developing trust:

The cause marketing program, which is designed primarily as a competitive strategy
The charity dinners
The golf tournament

Figure 11.7 combines both criteria—competitive advantage and building trust—in a matrix. The matrix analysis suggests that if the company wants to use its programs both to build trust and to sustain its competitive advantage, it would want to support and improve its programs with the Alexander Middle School, the Carey Settlement House, and the state park. The United Way, while not a program that contributes to a company's competitive advantage, is a program for building trust in a community. It is a respected agency that responds to important community needs. It is also an agency that provides networking opportunities and is thus a way to develop positive relationships. The cause marketing program may be a major opportunity to use a charity to sell products, but it does little in itself to build trust. The golf tournaments and the charity dinners do little, if anything, to sustain competitive advantage and build trust. The Allston Library and the Children's Cancer Center are caught in the middle. Supporting these agencies may enhance employee loyalty and community trust. The company may want to classify these as discretionary programs.

The usefulness of the matrix or a trust/competitive portfolio analysis technique

Figure 11.7
Impact of a Company's Community Programs on Building Trust and Sustaining a Competitive Advantage

BUILDING TRUST

		Low	Medium	High
COMPETITIVE ADVANTAGE	High	Cause Marketing		Alexander Middle School State park
	Medium	Golf Tournament	Allston Library Children's Cancer Agency	United Way
	Low	Charity dinners		

is that it sets out the options available to a company for setting priority decisions on the support of community organizations. It can promote discussion and further planning. Community programs can be reassessed or redirected to enhance their competitive value or trust. A company, for example, may want to promote its support of the United Way by personalizing its message of meeting the needs of children, which many companies are now doing to avoid the anonymity associated with the term "United Way." A company could increase the trust quotient of a cause-marketing program by linking the national cause with a local organization.

It is an excellent interpretive device. It clearly depicts areas for decision making. And it is a technique familiar to managers. It is an aid to answering trust and competitive advantage objectives, such as the following:

Reputation/trust objectives

Will the program enhance the reputation or trust of the company in the community?

Will the program promote positive community relationships?

Can the program be defended in the community as only one of two or three priorities of the company?

Competitive advantage objectives

Can the program assist the company in becoming a low-cost producer?

Can the program assist the company in differentiating its products in the marketplace?

Human resource management objectives

Can the program assist the company in attracting and retaining employees?

Can the program enhance employee loyalty and trust?

Can the program facilitate the professional development of employees?

More important, the portfolio analysis approach provides ways of improving the measurement of the benefits of community programs. Market research tools and reputational analysis methods, for example, can be used to strengthen the analysis of programs. They provide elements to benchmark a program; consequently, it can strengthen research into evaluating the results of a partnership or any type of association with a community organization.

But this points to the weakness of using a matrix of this sort to outline the options available to a company. It depends on judgments. Precise measurement tools are now not available—and conceivably, may never be.

However, all portfolio analysis techniques, as Michael Porter points out, lack objectivity.[10] They are based on judgments and therefore are subject to manipulation. But used over time, they can be a check on consistency. They are one more step in applying business methods to an ever-growing expensive company activity.

SUMMARY

Companies have many opportunities to use their community support programs to sustain the competitive advantage of the company and, at the same time, contribute to improving the quality of life in the communities in which they operate. To do so, however, they need to adapt experienced business practices to methods of analysis. They also have an obligation to improve the analytic methods used for assessing the value of the community programs to the company and the community.

NOTES

1. M. E. Porter, *Competitive Advantage: Creating and Sustaining Superior Performance* (New York: Free Press, 1985), p. 11.

2. A. Smithers and C. Marsden, *Assessing the Value* (London: British Petroleum, November 1992).

3. R. Seal, Foreword to ibid., p. 1.

4. M. E. Porter, *Competitive Strategy: Techniques for Analyzing Industries and Competitors* (New York: Free Press, 1980), pp. 365–367.

5. Smithers and Marsden, *Assessing the Value*, pp. 8–12. A description of how the company carries out its value assessment can be obtained from British Petroleum, Breakspear Way, Hemel Hempstead HP2 4UL, England.

6. Ibid., p. 16.

7. C. L. Marsden, e-mail to author, April 22, 1998.

8. Porter, *Competitive Advantage*, p. 11.

9. See J. D. Marx, "Strategic Philanthropy: An Opportunity for Partnership between Corporations and Health/Human Service Agencies," *Administration in Social Work*, Vol. 20, no. 3 (1996), pp. 34–41; J. D. Marx, "Corporate Philanthropy and United Way: Challenges for the Year 2000," *Nonprofit Management and Leadership*, Vol. 8, no. 1 (Fall 1997), pp. 19–30.

10. Porter, *Competitive Strategy*, pp. 364–368.

Part IV

The Social Vision

Chapter 12

Shaping a Social Vision: The Value Premise of the Neighbor of Choice

Successful companies need a business vision. It is a statement of how the company should be positioned in the future, and it is usually depicted in terms of earnings, market share, or product development.

There is now a realization that in order to achieve its business vision, a successful company must also have a social or what some companies call a community vision[1]—an analytical understanding of societal and community issues, their impact on the company, and strategies for achieving that vision. In other words, the new realities of changing societies discussed in this book make a social vision a mandatory corollary of a business vision—and the philosophical and value premise of the neighbor of choice principle.

The adequacy of housing in a community, public sensitivity to environmental damage, the status of race relations in a community, the inability of a local education system to meet a company's changing human resource needs, community insistence for increasing regulations that control business decisions, crime, drug abuse—these and dozens of other issues, concerns, and needs can interfere with a company's ability to grow or, indeed, even to survive.

A number of companies began in the late 1980s to explore ways of accommodating business goals with the new social realities. One is Monsanto. In 1989 Richard Mahoney, then CEO of Monsanto Chemical, announced that by 1991 his company would reduce emissions from its plants by 90 percent. Mahoney recognized that the public was becoming increasingly critical of corporations polluting the environment. He was aware, too, of the growing strength and numbers of environmental advocacy groups pressing for increased regulation of business. "Companies around the world," he told his employees, "are making it plain, both in word and deed, that plants operating in their neighborhood must be safe, not just for workers at the plant, but for the neighborhood as a whole. And they're right!'' he added.[2]

Another example: IBM decided in the mid-1980s to be a global leader in the computer industry. But its strategy, IBM foresaw, could not be separated from societal concerns and demands. It recognized, in other words, that the successful implementation of a global strategy depended on the goodwill of people and governments around the world. John Akers, former president and CEO, stated:

In today's global marketplace, it is just about impossible to separate a company's economic goals from its larger responsibilities to society. The needs and wants of IBM's customers, and the interests of our employees, shareholders, and people in the countries and communities where we do business is intertwined. Therefore, starting with a worldwide strategy and reaching every local IBM effort, we have an obligation to help improve the quality of life and to be a good corporate citizen. We believe this approach not only makes good business sense, it is also the right thing to do. Ultimately, it helps ensure the long-term success of the enterprise.[3]

What Mahoney and Akers, along with their successors, have put into place are two parallel needs of the modern company. One need focuses on the internal demands of the company—the demand to control costs and be competitive in a global marketplace. The other need takes into consideration the changes in the external or community environment. These are the changing expectations and the new role of the community in defining a company's license to operate. Each of these provides the framework for designing how a company can become a neighbor of choice (see Figure 12.1).

Guiding this framework is a social or community vision. It is similar to what Arnoldo Hax and Nicolas Majluf, leading theorists in strategy, define as part of a corporate philosophy.[4] Corporate philosophy, according to Hax and Majluf, ''is an articulation of the relationship between the firm and its primary stakeholders, employees, customers, shareholders, debtholders, suppliers, *communities and government*'' (my emphasis). They go on to say that it is ''A statement of corporate values—ethics, beliefs and rules of personal and corporate behavior.''[5]

The neighbor of choice concept, as I indicated in Chapter 2, defines corporate behavior. It is not a definition of the company's philanthropy or community relations program. Nor is it a strategy. It is a corporate-wide principle of how the company has to be positioned in the community. Companies without a social vision repeatedly run into trouble. Exxon's insensitivity to the public concern about our fragile environment not only proved financially costly but also affected employee morale and the governance of the company.

After spending millions to produce a cigarette targeted toward African Americans, R. J. Reynolds was forced to withdraw the product because it failed to recognize the heightened concern among African-American leaders about the relationship between smoking and the differences in death rates between blacks

Figure 12.1
The Social Vision and Its Relation to the Neighbor of Choice Principle

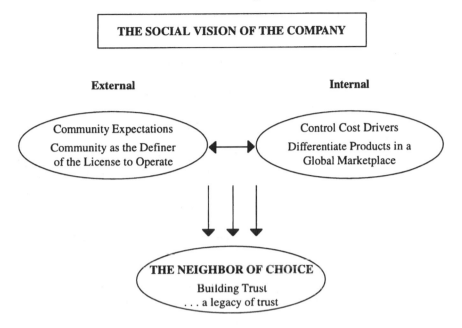

and whites. Its actions also refueled the movement to increase legislation and regulations against cigarette smoking, thereby affecting the future business decisions of all cigarette manufacturers. A social vision, consequently, is as important a part of a company's success as its business vision. The neighbor of choice metaphor is the means for carrying out the vision.

The implementation of a corporate vision results from the strength of the strategic intent and the behavior of the people in the company. It requires a clear and agreed upon mission and an executive group—CEO and senior officers—who are prepared to think in the longer term. "The successful implementation of longer-term business strategies," according to one author on strategic planning, "can only occur when executives are prepared to agree what the long-term will mean, to identify the actions required to bridge into the future and to debate actions which take into account the likely blocks to change."[6]

CHARACTERISTICS OF A SOCIAL VISION

A social vision has eight characteristics. They can be described as steps necessary for implementing the company's social vision.

1. *A purpose statement.* A social vision is a statement of purpose, an acknowledgment by the company that community issues have a direct relationship

to the company and its success. It is also a set of strategies, programs, and plans of action that are needed to achieve the social vision.

As a first step a social vision must be outlined and stated in the company's mission or corporate philosophy statement. It should be stated in terms of the company's recognized responsibility to the community and its commitment to being a neighbor of choice. The social vision statement needs to be widely used in the company's mission statements, annual report, annual social responsibility report, and internal and external communications.

Johnson & Johnson publishes what it calls the "Johnson & Johnson Credo," which describes the company's commitment and responsibilities to its consumers, employees, communities, and stockholders. Widely distributed to its employees, "The Credo," says James Burke, former president and CEO of Johnson & Johnson, "is a timeless document, idealistic in its goals but pragmatically effective when its principles are put into practice."[7] Burke credits the Credo with providing the ethical premise that allowed it to successfully respond to the Tylenol poisonings.[8]

The San Miguel Corporation, one of the largest industries in the Philippines and Southeast Asia, states its social vision in the following way:

Social Development is an integral part of San Miguel Corporation's corporate character. Our Social Development initiatives reflect our strong belief in contributing our fair share towards the improvement of the quality of life in the communities where we live and operate. By sharing the benefits we derive from society, our Social Development initiatives manifest our long-established and deeply held philosophy, "Profit With Honor."

We believe that Social Development should be pursued with a business perspective. Our Social Development initiatives reinforce our responsible corporate citizenship and transcend philanthropic endeavors, thus creating an environment conducive to business and economic growth. A healthy business in turn will enable us to carry on and even expand our Social Development commitment which will ultimately contribute to national development.[9]

Diageo, a holding company of close to 40 companies, including Burger King, Pillsbury, Green Giant, Bombay Gin, Christian Brothers Brandy, and Häagen-Das, headquartered in the United Kingdom, publishes its social vision statement in its corporate citizenship report:

Companies are one of the dominant social institutions of our time. The revenues of some already exceed the Gross Domestic Product of many nations. The exercise of this enormous economic power can inevitably exert a profound influence on the quality of life in societies all over the world.

This power for social good or ill is accompanied by responsibilities and therefore provides an opportunity for companies to ensure continued success by accepting and discharging these responsibilities. Businesses can make major contributions to societies over and above the satisfaction of customer and shareholder needs. It is in companies' interests to do so, because such contributions improve the quality of economic, social and physical environments in which they trade. Diageo Chairman, George Bull, has described this as a "virtuous circle."[10]

NOVA, the gas transmission company in Canada, uses a description of its social vision in a brochure called "Why Does NOVA Want to Become the Neighbor of Choice?" "For NOVA to successfully achieve its business vision, we must also have a social vision. This means we must understand community issues, how they could impact NOVA Gas Transmission Ltd. (NOVA) and develop strategies to achieve a balance between our business plans and the needs of the community. Achieving this balance will position us as the Neighbor of Choice and will encourage communities to welcome us as members."[11]

Chevron states it this way:

"Our vision is to be Better than the Best, which means:

• Employees arc proud of their success as a team
• Customers, suppliers and governments prefer us
• Competitors respect us
• Communities welcome us
• Investors are eager to invest in us

2. *The need for the social vision must originate from the CEO and be communicated by the CEO in word and example.* Only the CEO has the authority—clout, if you will—to insist on the importance of a social vision for the future success of the company. It is explaining the need for a social vision that is most important. If the CEO docs not spell out the relationship of the vision to the future of the company, and if the CEO is not personally involved in community relations, then the vision becomes a platitude.

One example is the much admired community relations program of the National Basketball Association. When David Stern became commissioner of the National Basketball Association in 1984, he inherited an organization that was the least known and least successful in professional sports. It was ignored by the major television networks. The championship games were broadcast on a tape-delayed format. Many of the franchises were in financial difficulty. Some were close to bankruptcy.

Since then, professional basketball has become an enviable success story. It is the fastest-growing professional sport worldwide. There are now close to 30 U.S. cities with NBA teams. With the support and assistance of the NBA, there are also professional basketball teams in Europe, Latin America, Africa, and Asia. An all-NBA team won the Olympics in 1994. NBA players are recognized in every country in the world. Major networks now broadcast weekly games. They also televise not just the championship games but also all the playoff games. They televise, too, the All-Star game and publicize the work the NBA players do in their local communities.

It is a great success story, due no doubt in part to the remarkable playing abilities of such star players as Magic Johnson, Michael Jordan, and Larry Bird. But credit should also go to the commissioner, David Stern. He brought marketing expertise to the promotion of professional basketball and rescued the NBA from oblivion. And one of the cornerstones of his marketing program was community relations.

Community relations, he insisted, needed to be an essential part of marketing professional basketball. As he explained to the owners, managers, players, and marketing managers, "We have a group of young men running around a gymnasium in their underwear. But if that is all we can show our fans and television audiences, we will not succeed in the long run. We have to demonstrate value beyond playing a child's game. We demonstrate that value by what we do in our communities," he insisted. "Our long term success," he explained, "depends upon our ability to demonstrate that we have a sincere and genuine interest in the communities in which we operate. To do that we have to make a contribution to each of our communities' quality of life."

This was not an easy concept to "sell" to the owners and players of NBA teams. Each team is an individually owned franchise, run often by strongwilled businesspeople intent on earning a profit. The coaches focus on winning games so that they can advance their careers and, for many, just to simply keep their jobs. The players concentrate on improving their skills, increasing their salaries, and hopefully extending their careers. Anything outside of these narrow objectives is obviously resisted.

Stern doggedly and persistently carried his community relations message to the teams. At the annual meetings, he met personally with the owners, urging, persuading, and coaxing them to establish a stand-alone community relations function. He asked the coaches and players to get involved in community activities, particularly in activities that would improve public education. He met personally with the community relations managers, only a handful at the outset, giving them support and encouraging them in their efforts.

He put the League office behind his message. He hired community relations personnel. He underwrote training for each of the teams' community relations managers twice a year. He provided marketing assistance and personnel to each of the teams in order to make their public educational programs a success. And he hired former well-known and -respected basketball stars to sell his concept to the players.

This was a personal effort on the part of the commissioner. But it paid off. From a handful of community relations managers, there are now stand-alone managers in every franchise. The involvement in public education has contributed to increasing the importance of education to children in the inner cities. Even more important, these activities have contributed to the public esteem of the players and their teams—not the kind of esteem enjoyed by other professional sports teams.

When asked why he thought community relations was important for a professional basketball team, Stern said, "I believe in it. We need to demonstrate that we can add value to the communities in which we operate. Otherwise we will fail as a business." Then he added with a smile, "I'm also an old fashioned Kennedy Democrat, and believe in the principle of giving back to our society."[12]

One of the results of Stern's social vision is that its community relations are the envy of other professional sports teams. For example, after the announcement that the National Football League (NFL) had negotiated a $17.6 million television contract in January 1998 with Fox, ESPN, ABC, and CBS, Warren Moon, the Seattle Seahawks' quarterback, said that the megabillion-dollar deal should prompt the League to be more charitable. "The league," said Moon, "which is making the bulk of the money, can do more to get closer to the community like the NBA That's why the NBA has grabbed the young fan. They do more stuff with young kids and schools."[13] Subsequently, one of the stipulations in the extension of the collective-bargaining agreement announced in February 1998 was that the NFL and its players will donate $100 million to a fund for the further development of youth football programs. Stern's persistence made a social vision a reality.

Another example. In 1985 Ian Rolland, president and CEO of Lincoln National, a nationwide insurance company in Fort Wayne, Indiana, met with a group of parents concerned about the racial imbalance of the school system. The school system had ignored a problem that had continued for years which affected the quality of the system and the long-term employee needs of the company.

The committee, composed of both black and white parents, consulted a civil rights attorney who advised the group to file a lawsuit against the school. Lincoln National financed the lawsuit, and, said Rolland in a speech at the 1989 Community Relations Leaders Conference in Washington, D.C., "we made no attempt to hide that fact from the public. In a community," continued Rolland, "where some residents still don't consider integrated elementary schools a high priority, it was not the most popular corporate contribution Lincoln National has made in its 84 year history."

For three years the suit was argued in the court and in the community. The company was both vilified and praised. Early in 1989 the risk taking of the company began to pay off. The school board voted to accept the racial imbalance plan of the parent committee, of which Rolland had become a member. The suit was settled out of court. Rolland's actions were guided by a vision that claims the company strives "to create an environment of mutual understanding and trust that will have a favorable impact on the corporations's overall operations."[14]

Ford Motor Company uses its community relations newsletter *Network* to stress the company's version of a social vision. Periodically the president of Ford reports in the newsletter on the importance and tradition of the company's community involvement. In 1992, for example, Harold Poling, the then-chairman of the board, said, "I want to . . . thank you for your volunteer service—a unique and enduring tradition—and to urge you to continue this worthy activity with a renewed sense of its importance.''[15] Alex Trotman, current Ford chairman, continues with the tradition and reports his views on community relations to Ford employees.[16]

3. *A social vision must become as integral a part of the company's culture as its business vision.* The social vision serves as a compass for management decisions. Major business decisions cannot be made without first reviewing the societal and community consequences of those decisions. Corporations, for example, must expect that a clean, healthy environment is a priority to everyone. Decisions that run counter to that expectation are fraught with peril.

AT&T, among others, views its management decisions against environmental consequences. ''Every time we engage in an activity—designing a product, purchasing a car, digging a ditch to lay cable or simply throwing out a piece of paper—we must understand the effect that action will have on the environment now, and in the future,'' says Dave Chittick, AT&T vice president.[17] NOVA, Merck, Olin, Houston Lighting and Power, and Ford Motor Company, to cite a few examples, have introduced community relations training programs for their operating managers to make them sensitive to community issues and concerns.

David Stern's success with the League adoption of a community relations strategy was due in no small part to making community relations a part of a marketing or business strategy. It became integral and therefore a natural part of running a professional basketball team.

4. *A company's social vision must be individually tailored to the company.* Industries have different needs and different impacts on communities. Oil, chemical, and pharmaceutical companies, for example, have sensitive and tenuous relationships in local communities. Moreover, they are governed by regulations that require community response programs far different than many other industries. (Although these regulations may be mandatory for manufacturing companies shortly.)

Consequently, companies in these kinds of industries must pay careful attention to the relationship focus of their community or social vision. Many do, which I have cited earlier. It is not an accident that oil and chemical companies are well ahead in the learning curve of designing programs that support a relationship-focused social vision.

Consumer products producers need to design a social vision and strategies that position their the companies favorably with consumers. Their social vision needs to influence their marketing and advertising strategies.

Local utilities must respond to a different set of community issues than global manufacturing companies, and regional differences will also come into play. Societal and community issues are different in California, for example, than in New England.

To tailor the vision to the uniqueness of the company requires study and analysis. There needs to be a planning format, described elsewhere in this book, that takes into account the needs of local communities, emerging issues, and the strengths of the company for developing a social vision.

5. *Companies need to allocate sufficient resources—human and financial— to achieve their social visions.* Between 1980 and 1990 corporate donations to charities increased dramatically. But a company's community relations efforts are more than just philanthropy, as I have consistently maintained. While donations doubled and tripled, the financial and human resources needed to operate an effective neighbor of choice program have stagnated since the mid-1990s.

Boston College Center for Community Relations survey reports show that salaries to community relations managers have not kept pace with inflation. In its *1997 Profile of the Community Relations Profession,*[18] the average salaries of community relations managers increased $2,715 between 1995 and 1997, or 4.1 percent. The rate of inflation during that period was 5.4 percent.

A comprehensive neighbor of choice program, as pointed out in this book, is designed to make a company competitive. It can also be a direct source for avoiding costs associated with failures to achieve community support or at the very least acceptance for business goals and strategies. Think for a moment of the costs that could conceivably have been saved by companies such as Disney, Shell U.K., Wal-Mart, and the New England Patriots if community relations resources had been used to assess community attitudes toward their plans.

6. *Implementing neighbor of choice strategies needs to be decentralized and become a responsibility of general managers at plant and facility levels.* Becoming a neighbor of choice is not, as was pointed out, a philanthropy, volunteer, or community relations strategy. It is a corporate principle. General managers are the visible and accountable presence of the company in the community. General managers, for example, are held accountable by the federal government for compliance with SARA Title III, the community right-to-know legislation.

Frequently, too, it is the general manager who can best understand the changing expectations of a community. The general manager's involvement with key organizations is a source of what is happening in a community. The Raytheon vice president for human resources told its company's managers, ''Community relations in earlier years meant attending Rotary Club meetings. Today it means such things as helping communities solve problems in the schools and adhering to right-to-know laws which require detailed reports to the community about business operations.''[19]

Merck's instructions to its facility managers and staff members are ''to get up from their desks, leave their facilities, enter their communities and interact with various people whom they (and/or their management teams) have designated as neighbors.''[20]

7. *Corporations need to increase the demands and expectations of community relations staffs.* When asked, CEOs repeatedly say that they expect the community relations staff to serve as the eyes and ears of the community. Their

association with other community relations managers and direct involvement in community activities lead them to be a valid and reliable source of information.

But CEOs are now looking to community relations managers to be more than the eyes and ears of the community. That is a passive role. They also expect them to be advocates of change in the company. Craig Sullivan, CEO of the Clorox Company, for example, expects his community relations staff to "bring about the change in our company that positions The Clorox Company as a neighbor of choice in every community in which we do business."[21]

Identifying and analyzing issues and becoming advocates of change, however, constitute only one part of community relations managers' functions today. They need to assume a very different leadership role in the company than the one to which they have become accustomed. Because the neighbor of choice is a responsibility of all managers, community relations managers need to be skilled in training and coaching. Merck now holds its community relations managers responsible for the design and operation of general managers' community relations training. Another responsibility that is increasing is the demand for planning skills. It is not enough to know which issues are critical in a community. The community relations staff must be able to put these issues into a planning framework and develop strategies for achieving the company's social vision.

One shift in practice, and one that will probably be the most difficult to bring about, is to decrease the public visibility of the community relations staff in the community. All too often in the past, community relations managers took credit for the company's programs. They were featured and quoted in news releases. The programs became associated with the community relations managers and not the company, which defeats the purpose of driving the social or community vision throughout the company. The company's programs should promote the company or the CEO, not the community relations manager.

The days when community relations responsibilities were limited to running the annual United Way campaign or representing the company at the museum luncheon are obviously over. Community relations staff who are skilled in planning, managing, evaluating, and promoting the company's programs and reputation in the community have become a necessity in today's corporations. This requires a new and more demanding role for community relations managers as leaders in their companies.

8. *Finally, there must be a recognition that the development and implementation of a social vision is the responsibility of a company's entire management team.* There is a tendency for senior managers, often at the vice presidential level, to resist the idea of spending time and money on community issues and programs. This reluctance is understandable. Most managers are comfortable dealing with questions related to achieving the business vision of a company— an idea drummed into them throughout their management careers. Few have experiences dealing with societal and community issues, and as a consequence, these issues become unimportant and unrelated to the success of the company.

But managers need to be convinced that corporations can no longer accept this kind of thinking. Today's political and social environment calls for a new approach to managing the corporation. Peter Drucker argued as much as early as 1980 when he said that the modern manager has to be a political activist. "Managers," writes Drucker, "will find increasingly that in turbulent times they have to be leaders and integrators in a pluralist society, in addition to managing their institutions for performance."[22] As usual, Drucker recognized the need for change and a new reality in the relationship between companies and communities.

By looking at this new role as a way of integrating a company's social vision into its business vision, managers will be better able to adapt managing today's corporation in turbulent times.

NOTES

1. This was first reported in the *New York Times*. See E. M. Burke, "Caring's Dollar Value," *New York Times*, February 18, 1990.

2. R. J. Mahoney, *A Commitment to Greatness* (St. Louis: Monsanto Company, 1988), p. 34.

3. Quoted in *1990 Annual Report, the Center for Corporate Community Relations at Boston College* (Chestnut Hill, MA: Center for Corporate Community Relations at Boston College, 1990), p. 8.

4. A. C. Hax and N. S. Majluf, *The Strategy Concept and Process: A Pragmatic Approach* (Englewood Cliffs, N.J. Prentice-Hall, 1991), p. 346.

5. Ibid., p. 341.

6. L. Gratton, "Implementing a Strategic Vision—Key Factors for Success," *Long Range Planning*, Vol. 29, no. 3 (1996), p. 290.

7. Johnson & Johnson, *People Helping People* (New Brunswick, NJ: Johnson & Johnson, 1995), p. 1.

8. J. Burke, speech to CEO Institute of the Center for Corporate Community Relations at Boston College, April 13, 1987.

9. San Miguel Corporation, *Social Development: A Corporate Commitment* (Metro Manila: San Miguel Corporation, n.d.), p. 2.

10. Grand Metropolitan, *Report on Corporate Citizenship, 1997* (London: Grand Metropolitan PLC, 1996), p. 8.

11. "Why Does NOVA Want to Become a Neighbor of Choice?" (Calgary, Canada: NOVA, 1996).

12. David Stern, interview with author, Boca Raton, FL, September 14, 1990.

13. Quoted in W. C. Rhoden, "Golden Goose Just Got Much Fatter," *New York Times*, January 17, 1998, p. B17.

14. I. M. Rolland, "Community Relations: Critical Business Strategies for the 1990s" (speech at 1989 Community Relations Leaders Conference, Philadelphia, PA, October 15, 1989).

15. H. A. Poling, "Serving Our Communities Is a Worthy American Tradition," *Network*, Vol. 6, no. 2 (1992), p. 1.

16. See A. Trotman, "Ford Honors Hispanic Cause," *Network*, Vol. 8, no. 1 (1994); B. Simmons, "Dearborn Development," *Network*, Vol. 11, no. 1 (1997).

17. Quoted in L. Whitefield, "Environment in the '90s," *Focus*, Vol. 4, no. 2 (February 1990), p. 31.

18. Center for Corporate Community Relations at Boston College, *1997 Profile of the Community Relations Profession* (Chestnut Hill, MA: Center for Corporate Community Relations at Boston College, 1997).

19. Quoted in the *Raytheon News* (Waltham, MA, October 1988), p. 4.

20. Merck, *A Guide to Becoming a Neighbor of Choice* (Whitehouse Station, NJ: Merck & Co., 1997), p. 7.

21. Interview with author, Santa Barbara, CA, March 16, 1998.

22. P. F. Drucker, *Managing in Turbulent Times* (New York: Harper & Row, Publishers, 1980), pp. 217–221.

Selected Bibliography

Ackerman, R., and Bauer, R. *Corporate Social Responsiveness: The Modern Dilemma*. Reston, VA: Reston Publishing Company, 1976.

Auguilar, F. J. *Supercharging Corporate Performance: Business Ethics in Action*. New York: Oxford University Press, 1994.

Avishi, B. "What Is the Business Social Compact?" *Harvard Business Review*, January–February 1994, pp. 38–47.

Blake, D. H., Frederick, W. C., and Myers, M. S. *Social Auditing: Evaluating the Impact of Corporate Programs*. New York: Praeger, 1976.

Bucholz, R. A. *Essentials of Public Policy for Management*, 2nd ed. Englewood Cliffs, NJ: Prentice-Hall, 1990.

Carroll, A. B. *Business and Society: Ethics and Stakeholder Management*. Cincinnati: South-Western Publishing Co., 1989.

Chappell, T. *The Soul of Business: Managing for Profit and the Common Good*. New York: Bantam, 1993.

Covello, V. T., Sandman, P. M., and Slovic, P. *Risk Communication, Risk Statistics, and Risk Comparison: A Manual for Plant Managers*. Washington, DC: Chemical Manufacturers Association, 1988.

Cutlip, S. M. *The Unseen Force*. Hillsdale, NJ: Erlbaum, 1994

Dilenschneider, R. L. *Power and Influence: A Practitioner's View of the Exercise of These Concepts*. New York: Prentice-Hall, 1990.

Etzioni, A. *The Spirit of Community: Rights and Responsibilities and the Communitarian Agenda*. New York: Crown, 1993.

Fink, S. *Crisis Management: Planning for the Inevitable*. New York: AMACOM, 1986.

Freeman, R. E. *Strategic Management: A Stakeholder Approach*. Boston: Pittman, 1984.

Friedman, M. "The Social Responsibility of Business Is to Increase Profits." *New York Times Magazine*, September 13, 1970

Grefe, E. A., and Linsky, M. *The New Corporate Activism: Harnessing the Power of*

Grassroots Tactics for Your Organization. Boston: Harvard Business School Press, 1994.

Hoffman, M. W. et al. *Business Ethics.* New York: McGraw-Hill, 1994.

Lippman, W. *Public Opinion.* New York: Macmillan, 1922.

Lundberg, L. B. *Public Relations in the Local Community.* New York: Harper, 1950.

Mitchell, R. K., Agle, B. R., and Wood, D. J. "Toward a Theory of Stakeholder Identification and Salience: Defining the Principle of Who Counts and What Really Counts." *Academy of Management Review*, Vol. 22, No. 4 (1997), pp. 853–886.

Nasal, J. L., and Julian, D. A. "The Psychological Sense of Community in the Neighborhood." *APA Journal*, Spring 1995.

Peak, W. J. "Community Relations." In P. Lesly, *Public Relations Handbook*, 3rd ed. Englewood Cliffs, NJ: Prentice-Hall, 1983.

Rauch, J. *Demosclerosis: The Silent Killer of American Government.* New York: Times Books, 1994.

Rheingold, V. *The Virtual Community.* New York: Harper Perennial, 1993.

Rubin, H., and Rubin, I. S. *Community Organizing and Development*, 2nd ed. New York: Macmillan, 1992.

Sandman, P. M. *Responding to Community Outrage: Strategies for Effective Risk Communication.* Fairfax, VA: American Industrial Hygiene Association, 1993.

Steiner, G. A., and Steiner, J. F. *Business, Government and Society*, 7th ed. New York: McGraw-Hill, 1994.

Taub, R. *Community Capitalism: Creation of an Inner-City Bank in Chicago.* New York: McGraw-Hill, 1994.

Name Index

Subject Index

About the Author

EDMUND M. BURKE is Founder and Director Emeritus of the Boston College Center for Corporate Community Relations. He has worked with over 800 corporations around the world doing executive education, consultation, and research. He has taught community planning in graduate schools of social work and worked as a community planner in Williamsport and Pittsburgh, Pennsylvania and Marion, Ohio. Dr. Burke served as Dean of the Graduate School of Social Work at Boston College. He was a member of the White House Domestic Policy Council from 1978 to 1980, and he chaired the White House Conference on Strategic Planning.